Tips From the
Cruise Addict's Wife

Tips, tricks and stories to plan the best cruise ship vacation

Deb Graham

Other Books By Deb Graham

How to Complain...and get what you deserve

*An easy-to-read guide to dealing with companies that don't
live up to their promises, getting you what you pay for.
Anyone who shops for anything will enjoy this book---and
learn how to get what you deserve!*

Quick and Clever Kids' Crafts

*Loaded with easy, classy crafts for children and adults. A
must for parents, teachers, scout leaders and anyone else
who'd rather see a creative child than a bored one*

Awesome Science Experiments for Kids

*Simple, impressive science experiments; a fun teaching tool
for adults to share with kids*

Savory Mug Cooking

*Easy-yet-impressive lunch recipes made with fresh
ingredients, cooked right in your favorite mug! Expensive
Take Out lunches—not anymore!*

Golf Tees and Rubber Bands

*Dozens of new uses for twenty ordinary household items you
don't think twice about. From using golf tees to hang your
hammer to dental floss for scrapbooking, you'll be inspired to
look around the house before you run back to the store.*

Tips from the Cruise Addict's Wife

Contents

I Didn't Plan on the Addiction...

You hold in your hands a very comprehensive guide to cruise vacations, with tips and tricks found nowhere else. The Bonus section has tricks for paying less than just about anyone else onboard, by the Cruise Addict himself. That's him on the cover.

I am The Cruise Addict's wife, but I didn't start out that way. Many stories weave through this guide, and here's the first one:

Our 20th wedding anniversary was coming up, and I wanted to do Something Wonderful. I had long dreamed of a cruise, a once in a lifetime adventure. I envisioned open seas, luxurious dining on an elegant ship, romance, ports of call to explore, time to step off the world and relax without the kids, a time to really celebrate.

Husband, normally an agreeable soul, balked. He imagined being stuck on a dinky, smelly boat for days on end, surrounded by hoards of people he didn't know. Miserable. Trapped. He complained to his buddy that his wife (that's me) had A Ridiculous Idea. He started to say, "My wife wants to go on a cruise for our anniversary--"Before he could finish his sentence with "—but I don't want to go--" the friend turned to his wife, who reached for the phone, and the plan was in motion, that fast.

Turns out her uncle was a vice president of Holland America Cruise line, and he had been suggesting they go on a cruise sometime. Steep discount in hand, the trip was booked on the spot for the four of us. Uncle even threw in a shore excursion!

To his credit, Husband fought valiantly. He DID NOT want to go on a cruise, no way, no how. Even that day, as we four drove to the port, he complained *non-stop.*   It was a 2 hour trip, and I'm telling you, he barely paused to draw breath. He used words like "shanghaied, " "forced against my will" and "railroaded" as he dug his verbal heels in. He clearly expressed his opinion that he would hate, *hate*, HATE cruising. But Husband loves me, and was frankly outnumbered. Amid his torrent of protests, he reluctantly boarded the ship.

Husband's transformation into The Cruise Addict took mere hours. Happily settled in the front of the ship with his high-powered binoculars, enthralled by the ever-changing scenery, fueled by diet 7Up and warm bar food delivered by a solicitous waiter, he morphed into a molten puddle of relaxation. Obsession was not far behind. I had no idea I had created a monster until I noticed Husband started most days by asking, "Can we book a cruise today? If I find a good deal, can we?"

Not _Exactly_ Once in a Lifetime

That once in a lifetime cruise has been repeated **many** times since that first trip. We have been on several dozen cruises on various cruise lines. Currently, we have four cruises booked (but, hey, it's still early). Husband (alias The Cruise Addict) has our travel agent on speed dial. He has become an expert on cruise ship, lines, tonnages, and finding The Best Deal Ever. The Cruise Addict even has all of our cruises on a spreadsheet, including the ship's details, the ports and traveling companions. It's probably a good idea; they tend to blur together, especially that one year when we took a record five cruises!

The Cruise Addict agreed to share his insights on **Finding The Best Cruise Deal Ever** in the bonus section of this book, so keep reading!

 Due to Husband (alias The Cruise Addict)'s tendency to brag, we have traveled with our kids, grandchildren, assorted friends, extended family members (both sides), various co-workers, Church congregation members, and in laws, as well as just-us-two. He has booked many cruises for our kids' honeymoons, co- workers, and friends, along with   friends-of-friends. I've often said, if he was paid $ 5 for each cruise he had a hand in booking, we could go on another cruise, paid for, outright. The dynamics of each cruise is different, some more fun than others, but hey---all of them are a cruise!

I Am Not the Cruise Addict

Let's be clear here; *I am not the addict.* I do, however, know rather a lot about cruises. I'm also a compulsive reader. I've picked up a remarkable lot of tips and hints. I've learned a lot! Some of it has been the this-is-what-you-must-not-do, let-this-be-a-lesson-to-you variety. I'm sharing it with you, all in one place.

 Besides being well-informed, **I'm rather frugal. Okay, face it, I'm cheap.** Part of the pleasure in a cruise vacation is the knowledge that I paid way less than the majority of people next to me, and I know for a fact I'm enjoying it more. I'd no more pay full price for a cruise than I'd pay book price for a new car. In the Bonus section, you'll learn how to save significant money on a cruise, both from me, and from The Cruise Addict himself.

Along the way, I'll share my tips for awesome easy cruise travel. Let's get started!

I recognize that not everyone travels as intensely as I do, but many of these tips in this book still apply to you. Be aware though, cruises are addicting! Don't say I did not warn you.

Who, Me? Cruise?!

Why Should You Cruise?

At any given time, there are approximately 200-210 cruise ships in service around the world. Figure each of these ships averages roughly 2,150 passengers, the size of a small city. More than 400,000 passengers are out here, right now, basking about on fabulous cruise ships. What do they know that most folks don't?

Cruises are a great way to vacation! The best part is the **flexibility.** You can book a one-day cruise, or 108- day around-the-world cruises, and a whole lot of options in between. You unpack once, and get a taste of a new place every day. On a cruise, you don't have the stress of we-spent-so-much-on-lunch-we'd-better-skip-dinner, or how-much-will-a-hotel-cost-tonight? Entertainment is built in, along with an organized plan to keep the kids happy. The constantly changing scenery alone is worth more than tranquilizers!

 A cruise includes transportation to different ports and cities. That's often cheaper than island hopping in the Caribbean or Hawaii. You can choose to spend as little per day as a night at a Holiday Inn, or run up a bar and bingo tab of over $10,000...in a WEEK. The cost includes all you need to enjoy a wonderful vacation. You can add on as you see fit with fancy drinks, shore excursions, spa treatments, specialty restaurants, casino, endless bingo games, and getting too friendly with the bar staff. Up to you!

Cruise Line statistics say fully **96% of passengers love their cruise,** and plan on taking another cruise. Where else can you get 96% of people to agree on anything?

Cruise Lines and Cabins

Cruise Lines Have a Personality

Each cruise line has its own personality. For example, Norwegian is laid back and casual and has the best suite perks in the business. Carnival is known as a party line, whereas Celebrity will be more sedate and has upscale food. Holland America caters to an older clientele, especially on longer cruises. I've never seen so many oxygen tanks and walkers! HAL is also the most traditional cruise experience. Singles fare best on NCL; the newest ships even have Studio cabins. Royal Caribbean is known for over-the-top ships and great kid's programs. Disney excels in entertainment and technology, although many people find their rotating assigned dining confusing. Disney's prices tend to be high, with few, if any, sales. Princess line caters to multi-generational families very well, and their staff is some of the friendliest I've seen. All cruise lines are in competition to make the cruise experience best for their passengers, with new innovations constantly coming down the pike.

Read up on your particular ship and cruise line for important details such as dress codes, policies, and itineraries. Most of the answers to Stupid Questions Passengers Ask are clearly detailed right on the cruise line's website, or in the brochures they send you once you've booked a cruise. Understand the demographics of the cruise line you are choosing to sail with.

Consider itinerary as you weigh which cruise to book. Are you looking for a laid-back sunbathing vacation? You're not going to like a port intensive cruise. Are you the kind of person, like me, who enjoys seeing new things and learning about new places? Interested in hiking and adventure, or are you out to shop? Figuring out your desires will narrow down your search considerably!

Which Size Ship Suits Me?

Newer ships have all the bells and whistles: some even have onboard surfing, water slides, rock climbing, ice skating, recording booths, even parades. They may include multiple eateries, and more shows than you can fit in your cruise. Naturally, they cost more than your standard cruise ship, but don't think the older ones lack for things to do! "Older" is relative; in cruise ship terms, anything sailing over a year or two is considered older.

Personally, I have zero desire to sail on one of the mega-ships. They are more like floating resorts, with the sea taking a backseat. If I'm on a ship, I want lots of places to hang over a railing, quietly watching the waves, not to be overstimulated by things such as Central Park. Isn't Central Park's atmosphere the reason I left the mainland?? Some of the mega ships hold more people than live in your hometown! I prefer seeing familiar faces all week, striking up conversations with them as we come and go.

However, I live with The Cruise Addict, so I expect a time will come when I reluctantly board a ship too big to even fit at a proper dock. Wish me luck!

Consider Your Style

I have a good friend who also cruises. Her idea of The Ideal Cruise involves staking out a lounge chair on an upper deck the first day with her four new books, and reading them all, surfacing only for meals and a once-daily trip around the jogging track. She sees no shows, participates in no activities, doesn't explore the ship, and speaks to others only at dinner, which she eats in the same place every night. Most of the time, she stays on the ship on port days, because she is engrossed in her book. She and I have been friends for 18 years, but we agree we can never travel together. Never ever. Ever! My style is...well, let's just say, more active. I deep down believe I may never get there again, so I'd better see and do it all. I'm on *vacation*—I can rest up when I get home!

It's nice to start off your cruise with a sea day, instead of a port. This obviously is not possible on all itineraries, but if you have a choice, it's great to have a day to relax and get your bearings before rushing into your first port day.

Choosing a Cabin; Options and Opinions

Extra Expense—worth it?

The couple staying in the penthouse cabin will be sitting at the same table, eating the same wonderful foods, visiting the same ports of call, seeing the same shows, and experiencing the same things as you. **They'll just be paying anywhere from 5 to 15 times what you'll pay.** Another way to look at it is … *they'll* take one cruise and for the same cost *you'll* be able to take 15 cruises!   Do you really need a butler?

 If you have a penthouse or even a full suite, you'll find you spend more time in it. You may not go to shows, or even restaurants, content to order room service…again. If you have a smaller cabin, you'll spend more time out and about, enjoying the ship's features, meeting interesting people, dining in new places. It's up to you---personally, I'm ON A SHIP, so I don't want to feel confined to a room, like in a hotel, even if the confinement is of my own choosing.

My brother's family went on a Hawaiian cruise a year before our family took the same cruise; same ship, same itinerary. He paid over $10,000 for the penthouse suite. For a *Week!* We spent $1900, for three of us, and booked an inside cabin, planning to spend our money in ports, exploring. We were upgraded to a balcony cabin for $190 (total!) just a week before the cruise. I know for a fact we had more fun than my brother's family!

Cabin prices are based on double occupancy. **Solo passengers pay a surcharge,** often 200%. You're better off finding a friend or family member to pay half the cost of the cabin. You do have a friend, right?

Inside Cabins

Inside cabins have a bad rap. Unless you are claustrophobic, **inside cabins are just fine.** If you are, you probably should consider a balcony upgrade an unavoidable medical expense, and do what you gotta do. Inside cabins are well laid out and efficient. Many people rave about how they sleep better in total darkness. They are often quieter, too, depending on location. The main selling point, of course, is the price. They often cost much much less than same-sized cabins with a porthole or window.

A nice feature of an inside cabin is the total darkness. Great for sleeping! It can be a little disorienting in the morning, when you're not sure what time it is or is it daylight yet. Before you go to sleep, **turn the TV tuned to the channel with the "bridge cam" or "view from the bridge," with the sound off**. You'll have a window to the world when the sun comes up.

Inside cabins are always smoke-free. Smoke can drift over from a nearby balcony, but if you're especially sensitive, an inside cabin is your best bet.

Families *can* fit in an inside cabin ---we've done it with two teenagers---but you have to really like them. We like ours. Rather than book a slightly larger Family Suite, **consider two inside cabins**, nearby or adjacent. It'll cost less, you'll appreciate having the extra bathroom, and they sometimes stay neater, too. Well, ours did...we booked a Girl Cabin and a Boy Cabin, with the appropriate gender parent and kid in each. The Girl Cabin was tidy all week. The Boy Cabin looked like something had exploded, and it was wearing a lot of clothing at the time.

Check the Deck

Before you decide on a cabin, **look at deck plans above and below the cabin you are considering.** Extra noisy places include under the pool deck (deck chairs at dawn), by the anchor, near the teen club, and above the theatre and nightclub. People tend to shy away from cabins near elevators, but we've found them to be quiet. Elevators tend to be separated from corridors by a fire wall, which acts as a sound barrier.

Cabins can be designated Ocean View, Obstructed, or Partially Obstructed. Again, **examine the deck plans, and those above and below the cabin you're considering**. Some obstructions can be minimal, such as a lifeboat hanging high above the window, or you may only be able to see a tiny slice of ocean if you crane your neck very far to the left. Decide if the cost is worth it to you.

If you opt for a balcony cabin, be sure to **check the deck plan before you book**. Some cabins are open at the top, unprotected from sun and rain. Worse, people above can look right down on you; not very private! Cove or Hull balconies are towards the front of the ship, where it curves. They can be closed partway up, or blocked on both sides by a solid frame, limiting your view a bit. The advantage is that some of the wind is also blocked, but of course, so is the view. Just be aware of what you're getting. Try doing an online search for that specific cabin number; people post pictures of just about everything.

A major complaint about balcony cabins is that cigarette smoke wafts over into neighboring balconies, or cabins, when the door is open. It's not a problem for the occasional cigarette...you just wait them out, but a cabin of three chain smokers can make your balcony unusable. **Smoking policy varies by cruise line**, so read up on yours.

Smoking on ships is a heated topic, and cruise line policies vary greatly. If your balcony adjoins that of a smoker, a **small battery operated fan** can prevent murder at sea, or at least increase the time you can enjoy your balcony without fumes wafting over.

Before you book a balcony cabin, **consider your destination's weather**. A balcony is a sweet treat in warm climates. How much time will you spend out there in the cold rain? Our first balcony cabin kept me awake; the door banged at every gust of wind! In Hawaii, we spent considerable time on the balcony.

If your cabin has a window or balcony, **be aware of your location at all times**. There have been numerous stories of people being intimate on their balconies, in full view of those on shore. Did you know passengers can be fined for that in some places?

Our ship was just pulling into   Halifax early one morning. I came out of the shower, wearing the appropriate attire for that activity, and realized with a start that Husband (alias The Cruise

Addict) had opened the curtains. I was shocked to see a worker on the dock, not ten feet from our cabin, eye level and looking right at me! He was also surprised, but he did manage a jaunty wave before I snatched the curtains shut.

We just don't spend enough time in the cabin to justify the higher cost of an expensive cabin. Mostly, we use it to sleep, shower, change clothes, and regroup. I enjoy being out and about on the ship. You can sit in a hotel room anywhere!

When Should I Go?

Booking a cruise out of peak time will net significant savings!
Holiday cruises always cost more than other times of the year.
Christmas, New Years, Valentine's Day are the more expensive,
and you can expect very full ships with many families. Think
about it—a major holiday with no one hosting or cooking for the
extended family could be a dream. If you plan it right, you could
even give shore excursions as gifts, and skip Christmas shopping
altogether!

Cruises often cost less between Thanksgiving and Christmas, in
early January, and after Easter, but before school is out for
summer.

**Cruises can often cost less on the beginning and end of their
seasons** in a particular area. These "shoulder season" cruises
may have iffy weather ---eight inches of snow in Alaska in May
comes to mind—but if you can be flexible, bargains are out
there!

Hurricane season can have great low prices, but it's a time
often disdained for cruise travel. People imagine being swept
away like Dorothy in the Wizard of Oz. Oh, wait, that was a
tornado. Whatever---have you ever heard of a cruise ship hit by
a hurricane? Of course not! In the event of a storm, the ships
simply detour around the worst of it. Yes, you may encounter
some rain, or even miss a port, but the ship will not purposefully

sail into a hurricane. They go to great effort to stay off the evening news. Go ahead and book your cruise.

Cruise "personality" depends a lot of **length of cruise, as well as time of year.** For example, a three-day cruise attracts younger people (they're often called a Booze Cruise, because that's the primary activity). Very long cruises attract retired-age people, because they are the only ones who can afford to take weeks off work. Cruises over Spring Break attract mid-20's, and holiday cruises (late December, Yeshiva week, mid-winter break week, etc) draw families with children...*lots* of children.

At some times of the year, the ships can be overrun with unruly children and teens. **The best time to go when there will be the least children** is right after school resumes. Parents will take their kids out of school for a vacation, but usually not right after the school year starts.

I have no tips on how to book around annoying adults, and there tend to be far more of them on ships. Bumbling humans are everywhere.

Before You Go

ID?? I Know Who I Am!

Get and carry a passport. You may sigh at the expense; it's just part of traveling these days.

Bring your passport for ID. Don't rely on a birth certificate, driver's license, Costco card, etc. With laws and rules and regulations in constant flux, a passport is the best assurance you'll have of boarding the ship. Every week, in every port, passengers are denied boarding for trying to use things like an expired state ID card, union membership card, cute little birth announcement his mom sent to her friends 34 years ago, and none of it works.

If you're going to Hawaii only, or a cruise-to-nowhere with no ports of call, you *can* board a ship with just a legal, certified birth certificate. In an unforeseen emergency, however, such as getting seriously ill or the ship breaking down and ending up in an unplanned port, it's a potential problem. You'd still need a passport to cross a border or take a plane home. The chances of that occurring are slim, but why risk it? Cruises are addictive, as my Husband can attest. You'll doubtless need a passport down the road. Might as well get it now.

Check to **make sure your passports are current**. Do this now. For international cruises, passports must be valid for six months past the last day of the cruise---don't cut it too short!

Double check with your travel agent to see if your **cruise itinerary requires a visa.** Contact the State Department well in advance to get the proper papers in order.

Before You Leave Home

We leave an **emergency contact list and itinerary** with each of our adult kids when we travel. I include the travel agent's phone, ship name, and how to contact the cruise line in case of an emergency.

I also tell them to avoid crises, calamity, emergency, mishap, and catastrophe while we are on a cruise. The point of my vacation is for me to relax, and coming home to a Problem shatters the mood.

Buy travel insurance. Don't go through the cruise line -- you can buy it less expensively elsewhere and it covers more -- but do buy it. You never know if you'll need a medical evacuation. Those cost way more than a cruise! I think it was about our 5th cruise before we had a whole trip without someone being evacuated off the ship by helicopter. We buy insurance if it's a costly cruise, more money than we wish to throw away (not for a $49 one day trip), or if it's planned far out. We don't know if we'll be expecting a grandchild in December two years from now, when we have another cruise booked . A new baby outranks a cruise, any day!

Traveling more than a couple of hundred miles from home? It's smart to **alert your credit card company of your travel plans**. The 800 number is on the back of the card, or on your monthly statement. If you live in Ohio, and the bank sees your credit card making a purchase in Oaxaca, your account can be frozen, in an effort to prevent theft or fraud.   It's a major pain to sort that out, especially from a village in rural Mexico.

Bring sufficient cash along, or plan on using shore ATMs. The **cruise ship will also have an ATM,** but the fees are high, since you are basically a captive audience.

 Traveler's checks used to be the safe way to go, but they are not accepted in many places these days. Use a credit card for major purchases to be safe.

Where Am I?

Ships Are Huge

Making your way around the ship, you'll need to know where the ship's front, back, and sides are. **Easy way to remember port and starboard:** *port* and l*eft* both have four letters. I do word association for stern and aft: ST*art* with the *stern,* whereas *aft* comes *AFter.*

To avoid the following exchange:

Passenger: Can you tell me how to get to my cabin?

Pool Attendant: Certainly. What is your cabin number?

Passenger: You mean you don't know, either??

Memorize your cabin number at home! Use word association, set it to a tune in your head, whatever it takes.

Read Reviews

Read online reviews of the ship and recent passenger reviews, as many as you can find, before you leave. CruiseCritic.com has loads of these, specific to your ship, as do other websites. Take these with a grain of salt. Make that a bucket of salt...because generally the people who write reviews either had a fabulous trip with no basis in reality, or a seriously lousy time. Many have nit-picky reviews, such as the waiter mispronounced their name, or their favorite Jell-O flavor was not available, or the glaciers looked dirty. Even so, read several, so you can get a feel for the ship. Do you see the same points made time after time? Pay attention to those. Don't rely entirely on the opinions of others; they might like to travel differently than you do. Remember my friend, with her books?

Keep Copies

Make photocopies of your passport, medicine prescriptions, return airline tickets, and emergency contacts to put in your luggage, as well as leaving a copy at home. I make sure any adult family members left home know where to access all this, should an emergency arise.

Passengers often **take a photo of these documents, or email them** to themselves so they can access them on a smart phone or internet on the ship if needed. In an emergency ---which is when you need the copies—I'm not trusting enough to rely on technology. You choose.

Go a Day Early

Get to the port the day before the cruise. Anxiety of watching a delayed flight draw too close to sail away time is not worth any savings you scored. Even a simple flat can tire ruin your vacation, if you don't allow extra time to get to the port! Instead, extend your vacation an extra day. $150 spent on a room and dinner the night before is well worth it to have a stress free start to your cruise. Spend the day checking out your new city and conquering jetlag. We have often seen passengers having to do the life boat drill on the first port day because their flight was delayed and they had to fly to the next port to catch the ship.

If you fly to a port, consider a pre cruise hotel near your home airport. Often, they offer stay-one-night-park-free-for-a-week deals.   Many hotels have a free shuttle to the airport, too. Ask.

When Can I Board?

Yes, you're anxious to board the ship! Keep in mind every ship is arriving back from a previous trip. The ship has to unload passengers, their baggage, all that saved garbage, and restock supplies. Check to see what time your ship arrives back in port as it's the same most cruises, except for unanticipated delays. When a ship arrives back at 7 AM, it's usually cleared by 10:30 and ready to board soon after.

Turn- around day is the busiest day of the entire cruise for the crew and staff. Often the cabins will still be being cleaned and made up when you board early. Public areas will be available, however, including the buffet. You may as well head to lunch; you've paid for it! Staff will greet passengers then point them towards the buffet.

Some cruise lines also have a dining room open as passengers board. That's a pleasant way to leisurely slip into your vacation mode. Don't overeat. Save room for the sail away barbecue, snacks before dinner, at least one dinner, double dessert at the buffet, oh, and do you know about the 24 hour room service?

You must be onboard at least two hours before the sail away on embarkation day. Some cruisers recommend **waiting until almost the deadline, to avoid crowds.** Yes, by then the mobs will be onboard. And yes, you will have had a few more hours in the city to explore, laze by the hotel pool, and wander aimlessly. I disagree heartily! You are there for a cruise, so get on the cruise ship, already! By the time the last- minute folks mosey onboard, you will have had lunch and a dip in the pool, explored the ship, unpacked, admired the artwork...AND you are more relaxed, already in Cruise Vacation Mode.

Get There Early

We all have talents, and I freely admit one of mine is worrying, specifically What Iffing. **If you check in early, and run into a snag, there's time to fix it.** If you have a dead credit card, or a passport/visa issue, isn't it wiser to allow time to handle it, as opposed to waving from the dock as the ship pulls out of its berth? On our first cruise, we encountered a massive construction zone that backed up traffic for close to two hours. We were so late, that a resounding FOUR passengers boarded after we did. Cutting it that close is just not good for my nerves. We have always boarded early since then.

I make a point of ignoring the recommended boarding time on the booking paperwork. For example, it may say 2 pm for an evening sailing. The lines to board are very long by then, and you already missed lunch. On embarkation day, the ship is cleared of last-cruise's passengers, then the new batch ---that's you!—is allowed to board, often before noon.

Early boarding gives you time to explore the ship and get your bearings before everyone else arrives. Okay, I admit I don't have a sense of direction, and I'm usually turned around on any ship until Day Three. But go try.

It's also the **best time to take pictures**, without others in the frame. You may not see the pool empty again all cruise long!

Once you've cruised on a line, you'll have **priority boarding** on subsequent cruise as part of the cruise line's loyalty program. This can be a good perk if lines are long to board, but you're not bound to the loyalty program line. By all means, choose the shorter one to check in!

Embarkation Day, At Last!

It's interesting to **watch your ship load on supplies** for your cruise in the embarkation port. I've enjoyed watching nearby ships do the same, often happily...oh, good, that ship loaded four pallets of instant mashed potatoes, and mine didn't!

Carrying On Your Carry On

As you check in, you and your luggage will part ways. **Be sure to have your passport, credit card, and boarding papers in hand**, or your luggage will have a nice vacation without you. The bags will appear in your cabin later in the day.

Pack a carry-on to tide you over, with the things you 'll need for a few hours. Medications, sunglasses, sunscreen, electronics, your passport, wallet, ID, credit cards, cash, along with anything of value, such a cameras, laptops, Ipods, belong with you, not in your checked suitcases. I always toss in a light jacket or wrap in the carry one bag. The upper decks can be quite breezy.

You don't have to put a **luggage tag on your carry-on bags**, but it's a good idea to do so. In your excitement of exploring your new home, it's easy to set the bag down. You stand a far better chance of it making its way to your cabin if someone knows where it belongs.

That reminds me... be sure to **pack your swimsuit in your carry-on bag the first day**, if you're boarding in decent weather. Your cabin may not be ready, your luggage may not appear for hours, but you can still get in a refreshing swim. Try not to smirk at those passengers who didn't pack a change of clothing. You know who they are; they're the ones still wearing sweatshirts from flying in from snowy climes.

Is My Suitcase Here Yet?

The cruise line has until late evening to deliver your luggage, although we find it's often much earlier. We almost always have time to unpack before sail away. On the unlucky chance your suitcase goes wandering, tell the Guest Services desk after sail away. In most cases, your suitcase merely went exploring the ship without you, knowing it'd spend the rest of the cruise under the bed.

If your **luggage really is lost**, the Guest Services people will do all they can to locate it, and provide you with necessities until it's found. I ran into a woman buying a heap of clothing in the on-board shop on Day Two out of Miami. She admitted "my bags are meeting me in St Lucia, so Guest Services sent me shopping!" Not to panic.

Check Out the Ship!

Exploring the ship the first day, preferably before everyone else boards the ship, is part of the fun of cruising. It's pretty sad to discover something wonderful on that next- to- the- last day, too late to enjoy the amenities. I heard a passenger complaining as we disembarked about the "lousy entertainment, just that one guy with a piano, night after night. " There was no point in correcting him at that point, or mentioning there was much more to see than the PIANO BAR! I've also heard of people who never found the dining rooms, just kept eating burgers by the pool every day. Fine, if that's your choice, but to not know what the ship offers is just ignorant. **Read! Explore! If that fails, talk to somebody**, for pete's sake!

To the Ship!

At the Embarkation Port

Keep all important documents with you, not in your luggage, the first day. You'll want your passport or other photo ID and cruise ship boarding pass in hand, so even if your suitcase misses the boat, you can get onboard. You'll also need to show your ship card and passport to get off the last morning. No, they will not let you stay onboard if you say you packed it!

Get your documents in order before you leave home. All cruise lines offer **online registration** these days. Use it! It saves so much time at check in. When you have completed all the documents, print two copies. One you keep in your carry-on you to check in, the other is in your luggage as a backup. We usually do three so that each of us has a copy in-hand, plus one in the carry on.

Fill out luggage tags at home, rather than scrambling at the pier when you should be admiring your first glimpse of the ship. Your last name, cabin number, and cell phone number is plenty...don't add your personal history.

Make sure you have the correct type of identification.
Wannabe cruisers have been turned away from the pier for
having just a photocopy of their passport or birth certificate, not
the required original. Your name on the passport must exactly
match the one on the ship's manifest (often a problem in the
case of a honeymoon cruise). Also, remember to acquire any
visas and immunizations necessary for your cruising region and
carry them with you. It's your responsibility to double check all
of your documents.

Look for coupon books in the embarkation port, as well as
when you leave the ship in ports. Often they offer significant
savings in port shops. Don't go nuts, though, in your haste to
save a penny; how many diamond crumbs does one passenger
need?

You'll be asked to fill out a Health Assessment form at the
port. It takes under two minutes to complete. Please be honest;
we've seen passengers who obviously had a respiratory plague
or worse on the ship, spreading apparent contagion. If you were
queasy as you board the ship because you ate four pounds of
fried mushrooms with habanero sauce last night, that's one
thing, but if you are genuinely sick, please be considerate of
your fellow passengers who are out to enjoy a vacation! You
also don't want to run the risk of what you think is just a mild
issue developing into a big problem at sea. This is a reason to
buy travel insurance.

Day One On the Ship

Don't be afraid to try new things. If you wanted things to be just like home, why would you ever leave? Being open minded and cheerful can make a real difference. Even if things turn out not-so-great, hey, you get a great story to tell for years to come. Above all, relax, enjoy the beauty of a different part of the world and be grateful you have the means to enjoy a wonderful vacation!

If you choose to buy one of the **all-you-can-drink soda cards** offered by cruise lines, wait until the ship leaves port, so you won't be charged tax. Decide first if you really drink enough soda to make it cost effective.

Ask for the **drink of the day** in a regular glass - they charge for those cute little specialty glasses (usually at least $1 more) and do you really need to take them all home? Well, maybe just a few.

Study the ship's layout before boarding. There is a handy deck plan on every cruise line's website. Be familiar in your mind the basics, such as where your cabin is located, dining room, pool, etc. You'll also be given a little fold out ship's map when you board. It's much smaller than the ones posted by most ship's elevators, but it fits in your pocket better.

Where the heck are we? An updated detailed map of the ship's route can be found near Guest Services.   Ships often boast a Bridge Viewing area with detailed routes marked, as well. I saw a man with a GPS system in his hand, out on deck, plotting his route. Clear case of too much time on his hands, in my opinion.

Muster Drill

You HAVE to go to the safety drill. Don't think you can hide out; they check every cabin and "clear" the ship. Roll taken, cards checked; they know you're not there, and they have the authority to make you do a make-up muster drill later on. Please, don't keep all of your fellow vacationers smoldering in the heat waiting for the crew to come drag you to drill. I read where Holland America removed some people from the ship that had attempted to skip the muster drill. They're only about 15 minutes long, and painless. Once they're over, your vacation begins for real!

Luggage and Luggage Tags

Some cruise lines ask you to **print your luggage tags** from home. You can print these on cardstock, which is sturdier than plain paper. I own some nifty little plastic sleeves that attach onto a handle. Mine were given to us by our travel agent, the one on speed dial. They're easily found online. You can "laminate" the labels with wide clear packing tape. Stapled on, or run through with a small zip-tie, those puppies aren't going anywhere.

If you are still concerned, **you can get regular tags at the departure terminal.** Just make sure you put your name and cabin number on them before you let the porters take them. Porters have notoriously bad handwriting.

Terminal porters rather **expect a tip.** We tip the porters $2/bag, in the hopes that they will make it to our cabin instead of going to Aruba without us. So far, so good.

Ever notice how many people have suitcases **that look just alike**? This can be a problem both at the airport, and after the cruise, when you claim your bags in the terminal. Tie a bright pompom, bold ribbons, wide fabric strips, or a vivid bandana to the handles to make yours stand out. I won't tell you what color to choose, because a sea of black roller bags with neon green bows isn't much of an improvement.

You can paint **a simple, vibrant design on your luggage** to make them unique. Use acrylic craft paint. Copy a very simple clip art picture, or make freehand swirls, flowers, lines, butterflies, whatever catches your eye. Not fish; fish are mine.

Colorful duct tape wrapped around the handles of your suitcases will make them stand out from others, and in a pinch, you'll have a ready supply of tape.

We've seen many suitcases with bold stickers and bumper stickers plastered on them. I notice them, because they are invariably peeling off. Your choice.

Photography and Photographs

Skip the formal photos, taken by ship's photographers. They're way overpriced. And beware that some are not standard sizes; custom frames cost more! Take your own camera, choose your own background and ask other passengers to take a photo for you.

OR

Pose for every photo op the ship offers. You only pay for the ones you buy, and you may just find The Perfect Photo. How often do you sit for a formal photographer? and when's the last time you posed with a guy in a giant seal costume?

Stock up on batteries, memory cards, film, and videotape for your camera before sailing, and bring your charger. Even if they have those items on board or in port – which isn't guaranteed – you'll pay at least four times the cost at home. If your camera can use rechargeable batteries, bring a supply of them and a charger.

Using a different SD card for each port assures your whole cruise's photos will not be lost should Something Happen. It makes it easy to remember where photos were taken, too, especially if you take a shot of the Welcome To (wherever!) sign. Some cruise lines even post the day of the week in the elevators. Take a photo of the floor mat or plaque that announces "Tuesday" first thing in the morning, and your photos are instantly sorted by day.

You could also **download the day's photos onto a laptop** or notebook computer each evening. I prefer multiple SD cards, labeled with masking tape, but it's up to you.

Take a million pictures. Take so many you feel silly. You will be looking at them all the time until you have the chance to smell the sea again, and your stories at home will be better with photos. You can relive your cruise adventure as you weed through them later. When I was a child, my mother would frantically exclaim, "oooh! You're wasting film!" any time we reached for a camera. With a digital camera, there is no film to waste, so take as many as you want, and an extra, in case your eyes were closed or you were speaking. Even if you are saying something charming, you'll still look like a doofus when photographed mid word.

Cruise ships passengers tend to be a friendly bunch---after all, they're on vacation! **Find a good background on the ship, and ask a passer-by to take a few photos of your lovely bunch.** I've never had one refuse yet. This works well in ports, too; ask touristy-looking folks. I find it funny that, invariably, they will take *three* pictures...they are as anxious for one to turn out as you are!

A hint: make eye contact with whomever you ask to take your picture. Husband (alias The Cruise Addict) one time asked a nice-looking man, standing in the atrium with his hand on his wife's shoulder, to take a few pictures of us. His wife looked stunned. He was *so honored*, he exclaimed, as he reached for our camera; no one had *ever* asked him to take a picture before. Turned out Husband had asked the only blind passenger on the entire ship to take our picture! The fact that the photo didn't actually include either of us in it isn't really the point, is it?

When you see a group a other cruisers trying to take pictures of each other in front of an attraction, offer to take their camera, make them all get into the shot and **take the picture for them.** Many families have thousands of photos, but none with Mom in them, because she's always behind the camera!

When you board the ship the first time, you'll doubtless be snagged by the ship's photographer. Cruise lines used to use real props, such a showgirl or railing with ship's name on a life preserver. Most have gone to using **green screen technology** for welcome aboard photos. They look great! except for people wearing green shirts, which simply vanish into the background. We saw some funny pictures of our cute daughter, with her smiling head floating over the Bon Vonage ship background, where her torso belonged. Looking farther, we found photos of happy people with palm trees sprouting above their waists, and city skylines where their stomachs belonged. You should take some time during your cruise just to peruse the photos---some are hilarious!

Bubbles

Bubbles!!! Bring bubbles so your kids (and you) can enjoy blowing them off your balcony or off one of the decks at the sail-aways. The kids will have fun doing it and you'll hear lots of others on their balconies laughing and enjoying it too.

Okay, I did hear a story from a woman who had brought bubbles for her children. As they blew them off their balcony, a large bubble went into a guy's drink on the balcony below them. He yelled at the kids and angrily dumped his drink overboard... onto a woman on the balcony below him. She started screaming. The family quietly retreated into their cabin, where it was nice and quiet.

Creatures at Sea

Look at the ocean! Gaze over the rail, watch the wake, that's the point of the cruise! You can feel your blood pressure lowering, by looking at waves rippling on as far as you can see. We've seen dolphins, pilot whales, orcas, flying fish, humpback whales, plus otters, tufted puffins, eagles, grey whales, leaping salmon—all for free, all right over the side of the ship! Flying fish are awesome---did you know they actually FLY? Until I saw them, I imagined flying fish would take a running leap and kinda hover until gravity grabbed them. No---they leap up out of the water and flap their little fins for all they're worth.

The passengers with their noses in their books missed out. Books have their place, I agree, but pages will wait. Nature is constantly changing. Constantly surprising, too. We had a wide window as we ate our dinner just before dusk. I spotted a dolphin, then another, then well over a hundred. It was a spellbinding show! Until a woman at the next table screamed "oh, come look!" and the entire dining room...did.

If you must be loud, please be informed... I still doubt that person loudly insisting as we watched pilot whales follow the ship, "they're Orcas! Orcas, I tell you!" was actually a marine biologist. Orcas are easy to identify, even from a distance; these were not orcas. It's a smart idea to **read up just a little on marine life** in the waters your ship cruises through. It's good to be able to tell the difference between a seal and an otter, and between a salmon and a floating log. Don't laugh; you had to be there.

Whale watching is especially good from cruise ships, if you are lucky enough to be in the right area. Ask a crew member— they know the route and where to look. The majestic animals breathe all day long, but feed at dusk and dawn. Look for mist against the distant horizon as their blowholes spout. Look a little longer, and you might see a whale breach or even spy hop. One morning, just at dawn, we saw a 40 foot long grey whale do a complete and total out of the water breach, then it flipped its fluke, close enough for us to smell its fishy breath. Awesome--- like a whale out of Central Casting!

Another time, we were playing shuffleboard on a lower promenade deck, and three humpback whales paced the ship, even with the shuffleboard court. They were less than thirty feet from us, so close we could hear them breathing! We watched them for about 25 minutes, until someone on the bridge helpfully announced "Whale! Starboard side!" and a stampede ensued. Ended the shuffle board game abruptly, too, as hundreds of people suddenly hurried across the playing area.

Small Public Rooms

Investigate the ship's Library the first day. Passengers are frequently surprised at the variety of books available to check out. It's easier than carrying a heavy book from home, and you might read something you'd walk past otherwise. Go early; by the second day, the good books are already picked over.

There will be a **book exchange** in the onboard library, where past cruisers left unwanted books. You may take them, read them, return them when you're done, or leave the one you brought to read on the plane, and the circle goes on ---for free!

Bored (how could that be?!)? The Library is the place to pick up a **daily crossword, Sudoku and word-search puzzle pages**. Free entertainment.

Look for the **Card Room** onboard. It's a quiet room with cupboards of board games and cards, free for the using. They usually have large windows and great views. For some reason, this room is usually underused on ships.

Get Involved!

Shows Onboard

Attend the nightly shows! A cruise ship's main show is different every night. I've met people who went the first night, then decided they 'didn't want to see a repeat the rest of the week.' Silly people!—the shows are different every night. The live production shows are a treat. Shows might include tribute bands, magicians, hypnotists, dancers, aerialists, comedians, even plays and musicals, all backed up by a live band. You've already paid for tickets!

Make time for the crew's talent show. It's often surprisingly entertaining! Some ships boast crewmembers from seventy countries or more. Combined---often amazing!

Activities in the minor venues are almost as much fun as the main evening shows. You'll find live music in many forms all over the ship after sundown! I avoid karaoke and think dance classes are just for watching, but go, if you like that sort of thing. Often, onboard comedians, dancers, improv teams, magicians, and the like will offer free daytime workshops. This is your chance to learn to foxtrot *and* juggle. Maybe not at the same time.

Take advantage of any on-board lectures and workshops offered. Well, I skip the shopping lecture, which is really more of a live commercial for select stores in the next port. But anything by a naturalist, or a local expert, is worth sitting in on. We enjoyed the slideshows and history lectures in Hawaii—it added to the trip considerably. You may never be there again...absorb as much of the area and culture as you can!

Jump Right In....

Make friends early. A good way to do this is to enter contests or sing karaoke on the first day there, or play games, as well as just greeting people. People will recognize you and start conversations. "Hi, is this your first cruise?" is a decent ice-breaker--- you at least have that in common!

Like **cheesy ship-logo prizes**? Participate in games, and tournaments. You'll have fun, and end up with mugs, coozies, insulated cups, key chains, books, t shirts, caps, pens and markers, photo frames, and other items you simply can't do without. At the very least, they're a fun diversion!

...Or Push Others

Passengers who are the most involved have the best memories. Smile and introduce yourself to the Cruise Director's staff early on. They are the ones in charge of passenger fun and games, participation-type classes, and some shows. Talk to them, greet them, be an individual. They enjoy meeting new people- -that's why they have that job. Cruise Director's staff tends to be very friendly, and they can help you out if you want something...like that tote bag.

You should know I'm very fond of tote bags. The Cruise Director's assistant was carrying a pretty tote bag, with the ship's logo on it...and I *wanted* it. I asked where she acquired it, and could I buy one? She said they were not available for sale, then a funny look crossed her face. She smiled slowly, "I see you like my bag. I need another Elvis impersonator for tonight's show. Make you a deal---get your husband to be my Elvis, and the bag is yours."   I glanced at Husband (alias The Cruise Addict), who was talking to someone a few feet away. I debated for a good long time, almost four seconds, then said "you got it."

Husband is not big on public performances, and his singing skills are less than professional. However, he knows every Elvis song by heart. Good enough, right? Not wanting him to spend the afternoon being nervous, I opted not to tell Husband that I had pretty much sold his soul for a very nice tote bag. We gathered for the show that evening with our three adult kids, a grandchild, a daughter in law, Husband's brother and his family, two nephews and a niece, Husband's parents, an aunt and an uncle. At that point, I did think that perhaps I should say something, but by then it was too late.

The Cruise Director's Assistant approached me, and grinned as she gave me the tote bag with a flourish. She took my very surprised Husband by the hand, and led him backstage. Three minutes later, Husband was belting out "Ain't Nuthin But A Hound Dog" like he'd rehearsed for weeks. For the record, Husband (alias The Cruise Addict) came in second place, likely because the first place winner had a voting bloc of a large real estate convention he was traveling with.

The only downside? Husband firmly asked me to never use the bag in public, for fear someone might admire it and ask where I bought it, and the Elvis story would come out. Don't worry, Dear, no one will ever know.

Moral of the story: Don't be afraid to jump into activities. Or push others, as needed.

Onboard Games

Your cruise will most likely host audience-participation games such as Trivia, Family Feud, Majority Rules, Minute to Win It, Pictionary, Liar's Club, Newlywed Game, Bocce, putting contests, and more. They're free--- just show up a minute or two early. Time and place will be in the printed daily schedule.

Get involved! It's fun to play with new people, and you might learn something about yourself. How would I ever know I have a talent for sucking up 40 cotton balls with my nostrils into a bowl in under a minute if I had skipped Minute to Win It?

The Cruise Addict and I are fond of Trivia games. Every ship offers them, often a couple of times a day. You'll need a team; right there you're meeting people. It's fun to stretch your vacation-logged brain, to see how much data you actually keep in there. Some games can be a little cut- throat, depending on participant's dynamics. After winning about eleven times in a row, a guy on another team pointed at us and shouted, "I don't care who wins—so long as it's not *them!*" Lighten up; it's a game. Prizes tend to be hokey, but competition can be fierce. We've seen people nearly come to blows over some questions. Lithium; is it a heavy metal, or an element?

Cell Phones and Key Cards

Part of a great vacation for me involves **symbolically stepping off the world.** I happily park my cell phone in the cabin's safe first thing, only removing it in ports. It's a smart thing to do...you don't want to run up astronomical charges for using a cell phone on the ship, or have to keep track of the darn thing. You can run up roaming charges just for leaving it on, even just to tell time. At sea, ships are their own cell towers. Unless you are high on the transplant list, few calls are so important that they can't wait until you step on dry land. It's a vacation! Vacate, already!

In an emergency, such as you- simply-have- to- tell-Katie- you-saw- your- first- whale, know that **text messages cost much less than a cell phone call** from the ship. Still more than at home, but less than a call. Cell calls can be at least $2.50 a minute from the ship.

Key Cards

Every cruise line calls it something different; some are passes, or sail cards, or ship key cards. By whatever name, it's the credit-card sized plastic card given to each passenger upon check in on embarkation day. **You'll want to keep your key card with you wherever you go**. It's used for opening your cabin's door (same as a hotel key), like a credit card for all onboard purchases (drinks, items in shops, magician's CDs, all of it), and you'll have to scan it every time you board or leave the ship.

A key card has a magnetic strip, which a cell phone kills on contact, every time. I refuse to carry a purse; if I have to keep track of anything that heavy stuck to the end of my arm, it had better be calling me Mommy. At home, I keep my cell phone in my pocket, along with keys, and a slim rubber -banded bundle of necessary cards and cash. On a ship, I also slip my onboard key card in a pocket. If you forget, and deactivate the card with a cell phone, the Guest Service desk will replace it for you. You can avoid another line by either jettisoning the phone, or using separate pockets. There's also the embarrassment factor...one of us, who'd prefer to remain nameless, killed a record FIVE key cards on one cruise. I may have mentioned I keep *my* cell phone in the safe.

Wait...did the Cruise Addict's Wife say she does not carry a purse?? True**! I've investigated how other women manage to carry their key card.** Ideas range from shirt pockets, wallets, in a shoe, inside a bra, in a friend's pocket (why don't all women's clothes come with pockets??), those tacky plastic holders that go around one's neck and carry a passport, coiled key fobs that clip on a waistband, a tiny clutch purse , retractable badge reels, lanyards, etc.

I personally think anyone over the age of six and not attending day camp is too old for a lanyard, but that's just me. If you do go this route, or if you are indeed six years old, know that the Guest Service's desk has a **hole punch for your card** to slip on your lanyard. For that matter, so does anyone on the ship who owns a desk; ask at the future-cruise office, or security, or library.

Magnetic closures on purses can also kill a key card...so I've heard. Does your camera case have a magnet?

Onboard Details

Internet

Internet connection is very costly, and ridiculously slow on ships. Instead, seek an internet cafe in port. Crew members know where they are located; they use them to email and Skype their families. You might be lucky enough to find a public Library in port, where you can **access your e-mail for free**. Ask!

 If you absolutely MUST get online on the ship, wait **until the first sea day to buy an internet package**. The daily schedule comes with many ads, and will usually have a 50% off sale. You can use the minutes you buy for the rest of the cruise. Prepare to wait, though; onboard internet is glacial speed, and I don't mean the global warming variety.

Ask crew members where the best WI-FI hotspots are in port.

Dress Code

Yes, it's your vacation, but please **be respectful of cruise line dress codes**. Just as you would not wear a swimsuit to the mall, or grungy shorts to a wedding, it's courteous to dress for the occasion at hand. Your cruise packet will detail what is expected, and I'm sure you already own most of it! Dress appropriately for a day onshore. Resort Casual is just fine all day, all over the ship, and for most evenings as well. Men will do well for dinner in a collared shirt and slacks, while women look fine in a simple sun dress or slacks with pretty tops. None of these take up much room in packing, so that's not an excuse. Some cruise lines have Formal Nights. Some passengers do dress to the nines, with men in suits or tux, and women in cocktail dress or better. Regardless of the weather, guys in baseball caps with hairy armpits and tank tops are never appropriate on a cruise ship. We have to look at you, you know!

Pack for your destination. Yes, you need a swimsuit for the Cayman Islands, and warm layers for Denali in September, flip flops for a day at the beach, gloves for glacier-watching, and you'll want your most comfortable shoes for long days sightseeing in port. Active excursions like hiking or biking require closed-toe shoes, and water bottles. Even if you're going somewhere warm, pack socks so you don't miss out on the onboard trampoline, climbing wall, or zip lines you may encounter.

Weather is not the only consideration. **Some destinations are more formal than others**. Americans know how to dress to the nines, but face it---we tend to be a casual lot. Being aware of what's expected wherever you go will make you more at ease. If you're touring Old World churches, women will be expected to have covered shoulders, perhaps even a head covering. I didn't feel very classy with a tissue bobby-pinned to my hair in Mexico! European museums and churches---even some in the Caribbean---don't allow shorts on anyone older than a toddler.

My friend carefully chose a skirt when she visited the Vatican. The guides declared it was too short, and insisted she pull her skirt down to graze her knees. I don't understand how a bare midriff with flowered panties on display is more modest than an exposed knee, but when in Rome, as they say.

Shipboard Behavior

Don't be a jerk. Just don't do it. Remember to be nice to all and sundry and you'll be a lot more pleasant to be around. In return, people will treat you better. Some people wear an Entitled Attitude on a ship, loudly proclaiming, "I can do whatever I want. I paid for this cruise, you know!" Actually, they did not...they just paid to be on the ship, same as every other passenger. Cruise ships are public venues. Your Mother was right---use your manners. Don't brag, hog pool chairs, monopolize conversations, shove people at elevators, make loud judgmental comments, run people over, be demanding, order the staff and crew around, or be obnoxious in any form. Think of others! It's their vacation, too.

Some **ship's cabins have paper thin walls**; at least it sure sounds like it! The family in a neighboring cabin had a baby, a cute little girl, maybe nine months old. We had no problem with her, not even when she woke up with a single squawk at 3am every night. I'm a mom; I understand babies need care. By all means, meet their needs---but I gotta tell you, by the fourth parental rendition of Itsy Bitsy Spider *every single night* at high volume to an apparently silent child, it was tough to suppress violent thoughts. Just think of others. Not everyone enjoys Itsy Bitsy Spider as much as you might think.

Smile and say hello to everyone you see. It's amazing how catching a smile is. **There will be enough complainers on the ship; you don't need to join them.**

Don't leave your manners at home. Most people we've met on cruise ships have been delightful, and added to our enjoyment, but there are always those few. ..I'm sure they act like that at home, too.

A cruise is an adventure unlike any other vacation, so keep cool and cheerful. A smile is truly the international language, so do this often on your cruise. Be kind, patient, and gracious with the cruise staff, too. They can make your cruise so much better if you are respectful and interested.

Traveling with people you're not particularly close to? Arrange to meet for dinner, and use daytime for free time. Or, you may be surprised to learn you actually enjoy being with them, now that they're relaxing on a cruise ship.

Ask questions. Don't worry about sounding silly. Why miss out when you could just ask "where are all those people going?" or "what does this mean here in the daily schedule?" or "where is the theater?"

Take time to enjoy the quiet times aboard the ship: a walk around the deck before you go to bed, an early morning sunrise, watching the ship's bow break the waves, or finding a seat in a quiet lounge during the day to read a book while sipping a soft drink and enjoying the ocean rolling by, is very good for the soul.

Security Onboard

Don't be afraid. Thousands of people are on cruise ships around the world at any given time, and very few end up on the evening news. Just be prepared, well read, and take obvious safety precautions. It's a floating city; don't do risky things like let your kids wander unaccompanied, or teens go into other people's cabins, or leave valuables lying around, etc. In other words, pack your common sense.

Use your cabin safe! Just don't tempt fate by leaving valuables out and about. You can program the code yourself. Pick an easy one that no one else can guess. A pattern, such as diagonal numbers on the keypad, works well, as does your mother in law's house number. Like any other passcode, don't be obvious; your cabin number is the first thing anyone will try!

Be careful with items of value. In an average day, your steward will be in and out of your room at least twice, along with the bar staff person who's checking your mini fridge, and random people like maintenance folks. Any of these could prop open your cabin door while they go to get something, leaving your belongings vulnerable. Use your room safe, or hide valuables in your suitcase, not in plain view. Most people are honest, but why tempt them?

And of course **keeping track of your valuables** anywhere on the ship is smart, just as you would at home. Don't leave your camera, e-reader, or two-year-old unattended anywhere.

I place our **cell phones, extra SD cards, passports, money, wallets, and small electronics in a large clear zip lock bag** before they go into the room safe. It prevents rooting around in the back corner in the dark to be sure you have it all. It's also a safeguard in an emergency. If I had to, I could simply grab the baggie and have the most important stuff in hand. Oh, yeah, I'd grab family members, too.

Onboard Credits

Onboard credits (OBC) are commonly offered as part of the get-you-to-book-with-that-cruise line ploys. These can be offered as you use certain credit cards, as part of a promotion for specific sailings or itineraries, as gifts from travel agents, and numerous other routes.   On some cruise lines, you can use this onboard-only money for anything you'd spend on the cruise, such as specialty restaurant meals, tips, shop purchases, drinks, bingo, and casino; anything you'd swipe your ship card for. Some limit it to tangible purchases only; your gift shop perfume is covered, but it doesn't count for gratuities.

 Unspent OBC is usually not refunded. You have to spend it onboard, a use-it-or-lose it proposition. This can lead to some silly problems. On a recent cruise, we still had $75 in onboard credit to use up, and could not use it for gratuities. We don't gamble, detest bingo, were full of virgin peach daiquiris, and nothing else appealed to us in the onboard shops. We had to spend the money, or lose it. We opted to eat at another specialty restaurant; that would use up $50. I happened to find a substantial piece of plastic in my seafood chowder, a piece of scallop's packaging, to be precise. I brought it to the waiter's attention, just so he could check the rest of the soup in the kitchen. Instead, he apologized profusely, and comped both of our meals! We protested, "no, please, that is not necessary!" He insisted, leaving us to find another way to squander our onboard credit. For a frugal soul, it was harder than it sounds!

Just Married!

Just married? You should also **tell your steward, and everyone else, it's your honeymoon.** People will be extra nice; we all love a love story. Odd freebies might befall you, such as drinks, and specialty dinners. Two of our kids cruised for their honeymoons, separately, obviously, and actually wore tee shirts with Just Married printed on the front. Shout it to the world! However, do NOT volunteer for the onboard Newlywed game. Go watch it...but it's highly embarrassing and not worth the prize. I did warn you!

If you are honeymooning, you need to **make cruise reservations in the name that matches your passports**, not your "married" name (if you're changing your maiden name). Your paperwork must match your identification, or one of you will be going on your honeymoon alone.

Since the reservation would look like two people with different last names will occupy the cabin, your cabin would be set up **with twin beds**. None of my business, mind you, but on a honeymoon, you may not find that ideal. Your cabin steward is out to make you happy, so you'll simply tell him you want one bed, together, please, and it'll be fixed before you're back from dinner.

Read All About It!

You need to be the most informed person on the ship, so as not to miss anything important. You'll get "mail" on the bed every night, telling the ship's schedule for the next day, which you may either participate in or ignore. Read it anyway.

The onboard schedule page has things you might want to know. It lists what time you can get off in port, what time to be back onboard, dining times and venues, information about workshops, demos, evening shows and where live music will take place. You'll also receive a heap of ads for ship shops and spas. I consider those round file fodder.

You will receive a **daily schedule** for the following day in your cabin each night, but just one. If you want extras, you can pick another one up at or near the Guest Services desk.

Bring a highlighter—or one color for each family member, if you wish—and take a couple of minutes before bedtime to look over tomorrow's **ship's schedule**. I highlight whatever appeals to me. I also pencil in the margin other things that I want to remember, such as the past cruiser's cocktail party, dinner reservations, and time we agreed to meet our friends for lunch. Folded into a pocket, it's a handy reference.

Read even small things, like bar receipts. Of course, it's expected you'll tip someone who brings you a drink, but look closely. There's already a 15% tip added! Spa services are similar, but the gratuity may be up to 25%. By writing in a tip on the line provided, **you're double tipping.** Go ahead, if you want to, but it's certainly not expected.

A Fear of Missing Something?

We were sitting on deck under a magnificent sunset on the first port day of the cruise, with four couples we had just met. We talked about how-was-your-day and what-did-you-do, as the ship sailed out of port. That couple had been shopping at boutiques, another went hiking, two of them enjoyed a whale watching tour, we had enjoyed three museums and a nice lunch... like that. One couple was silent, then finally burst out, "wait---you mean we can GET OFF the ship??" The next day, we saw them in the very front of the line to go into port, first thing. You may pick and choose, but at least know your options!

Have you heard the story about the school teacher who failed to read up on the cruise line's dining policy? She had scrimped and saved for years to go on her once in a lifetime cruise vacation. Determined not to go over her meager budget, she filled a suitcase with non-perishable food; cans of tuna, dried fruit, crackers, granola bars. On the ship, she'd walk longingly by the buffet, and trays of sweets, and the pool deck grill. Her mouth would water at the aromas wafting from the dining rooms, but she never once entered, determined not to spend a penny on food. Back in her cabin, all alone, she ate her crackers. It wasn't until weeks later, at home that an astonished friend told her she had missed out, that the buffet, grills, and dining rooms were included in her cruise price! Either **be very informed**, or take a friend who can read along with you.

Seriously, **be the most well-read person on the ship.** If you ignore papers, you will miss out on large and small things.   On some ships, ice is by request only, and even the fruit basket has instructions; fill out the form indicating which fruits you prefer, or it stays empty. You never know when you might want a crimson pear in bed.

Living in a Stateroom

Not Like Camping

Your cabin will be small, but very efficient. Here are some tricks to make it even more usable.

Battery operated candles add a nice glow to the cabin, and can act as a nightlight. Avoid them on balconies; it sends the Security force running. They look like real candles from any distance, and open flames are forbidden on ships! Remember if you can see the bridge, the officers can see you, too.

"Reasonable" musical instruments are permitted on ships, at least until your neighbors complain. Guitars, harmonicas, flutes, instruments like that, are good ideas. Tubas, trumpets, accordions...not so much. A friend of ours said the highlight of his first cruise was strumming his guitar on the balcony in the nude. He reported "my neighbors even applauded when I stopped playing!" Did he play well, or badly, or was it his outfit? You decide.

Every cabin has a **Do Not Disturb sign** in one form or another. Use it! You cabin steward will make up the stateroom twice a day, and often it seems they have ESP, knowing when you are out and about. Not always. We were almost back to our cabin when we heard a heated exchange down the corridor. Seems the passenger had left out his Make Up Room card, and gone to take a nap. The unsuspecting steward opened the door, and was startled to see a naked guy sprawled out on the bed. The passenger received a stern scolding. Deserved it, too. Use the card!

Bathrooms

Most bathrooms in the cabins are *small*. If you're of normal height or more, you'll find your knees often hit the wall opposite the toilet.   Tall passengers may have to do their business sidesaddle. There's nothing wrong with simply availing yourself of the public restrooms all around the ship. They're larger by far, and have better ventilation, too.

The mirror over the desk, not the one in the bathroom, is often **brighter for applying makeup**, and frees up the bathroom for your cabin mate to shower at the same time.

Many people suggest bringing an air freshener for bathroom odors. Our rule is: **don't poop in the cabin's bathroom.** *Just don't.* Our son- in- law-to- be was surprised to learn of this rule, but he's a good sport. The public restrooms are plentiful on ships, and have far better ventilation.

 If you do opt for an air freshener, pick a neutral scent.

Bring a **few clothes pins or large binder clips to prevent the shower curtain from getting too friendly.** Those showers are small! I heard a comedian onboard joke that he simply soaped the walls of his shower, and spun himself clean. A little added weight at the shower curtain's hem will prevent unwanted grabbing.

Showers in the workout/spa area are free for use by any passenger. They are bigger than the one in your cabin, which is handy for shaving legs, and come with nice-smelling amenities, too. Keep this in mind on days when all of you want to shower and get gorgeous for dinner, and you only allowed twenty-two minutes total. Oh, and for the sake of the rest of us, please wear clothes both coming and going. Thank you.

Shoe Holders---Are They For You?

Many people swear by **over the door clear plastic shoe holders**, the ones with individual compartments. The pockets can hold sun screen, sun glasses, excursion tickets, cards, hair care products, makeup, camera, extra SD cards or film, batteries, charger cords, daily ship "mail," brochures, maps, brush/comb, first aid items, prescriptions, note cards and pens, small cash for tips, pens, stamps, postcards, book light, lotions, itineraries, receipts, snacks, and as a last resort, flip flops on the bottom level.

I bought a shoe holder, after hearing how versatile they are. It took almost one day to grow more irritated than I could bear. We knocked it off the door every time we left or entered the cabin. It slammed every time the bathroom door was closed. Taller items jumped out of the pockets onto the floor, over and over. We quickly decided it was more in the way than helpful, and threw it away. Our cabin steward helpfully retrieved it from the trash and hung it back up. He even put our things back in the pockets. *Three days in a row!* I guess he thought we needed it more than I did. I finally threw the holder away in a public restroom trash bin.

Ship's walls are metal. **I bring magnets to stick notes** and tickets and receipts on the cabin walls. Some magnets have clips or hooks; even better!

Binder clips are handy to keep your curtains closed in case they sway with the motion of the ship, so you can sleep in past sunrise. If you forget, use one of the clip-type pants hangers from your closet, or a clothespin. Binder clips are also useful for corralling papers at the end of the trip. Papers multiply on ships, I don't know why.

Take some **suction cup hooks** to use on smooth surfaces. You can hang hats, scarfs, bags, etc. out of the way in corners or other unused space in the cabin.

Missed an urgent Ship's Shopping Lecture? Never fear...it'll **be replayed over and over on your cabin's TV.** So will that game show, the one where you made a complete fool of yourself, and some of the shows onboard. Many cruise lines broadcast a brief 'talk show' every morning featuring the Cruise Director, highlighting interesting things about the ship and the day's plan. It's worth the 10 minutes, while you're getting dressed.

Communication

Did you know that **dry-erase markers** work on mirrors? It's a quick way to leave a message for your cabin mate or steward. It wipes off easily. Just remember that your lovey-dovey may not be the only one to read it. Leave the mushy stuff for later; your cabin steward does not need to know you think she's hot stuff.

Use post-it notes to leave messages for your cabin steward, such as "We need a sharps container, please" and "thanks for the extra pillows." We also leave notes for one another; "Gone to work out" and "meet at pool at 2pm." The mirror is a good place to post them, because no matter how cluttered the desk may be, the mirror is always clean. So far, the steward has not met us at the pool at 2pm.

Cruise ship's walls are metal, so it's easy to stick the Plan For The Day on a wall or door with a **magnet.** I know people make spreadsheets and post them...even I have my limits.

Dirty Clothes Happen at Sea, Too

There is a little clothesline in the shower in every cabin. **Bring a few clothespins** to hang damp swimwear.

Don't hang clothing on the balcony. A cruise ship is a classy place. Don't make it look like a tenement with strings of drying clothing. Your neighbors would be surprised to inherit your dainties when the wind carries them off your balcony and onto theirs. Some environmentally protected areas have stiff fines for throwing items into the sea, and your laundry flying overboard is in this category. Don't risk it!

Stain sticks can save your outfit for another day. Blot right away when the salad dressing attacks your shirt. In most cases, spots disappear. At the least, it's a pre-laundry treatment for when you get home. **Baby wipes** rubbed on a fresh stain often take it right out. **Pre-wash wipes** are also good to have, if you are the kind to attract ketchup to your front.

Those flat, dry, all-in-one **Purex laundry sheets** are a lifesaver for rinsing out minor laundry onboard. Cut into quarters, then fill the sink. **Shampoo or the mystery soap** in the dispenser is also good in a pinch. Both are designed to remove body oils, so most stains wash right out.

Improvise a washer for small items. Use a gallon-sized or bigger zip bag with some detergent and water. Fill partway with soapy water and item of clothing; seal with air in it, then shake violently, preferably in the shower stall.   Rinse, wring out, hang up.

Need help wringing out larger items, such as slacks or a shirt? Enlisting a cabin mate's help is best, but this also does the job. Lay out a big towel, and place the item on top. Roll the wet item and towel lengthwise, then stand on one end of the towel while twisting it as far as you can. If you are careful to lay the item out flat before you begin rolling from the sides, lining up the seams, it ends up almost smooth, as well as damp. Hang carefully, after a light shake, and wrinkles will be minimal.

Those late night infomercials are not *all* hype. Those **ShamWow! super absorbent cloths can be a handy thing** on a ship. Get it wet, then just squeeze it dry. It sucks water from clothes you rinsed out in the sink, and wet swim suits. They dry much faster. You can also use it to blot yourself off when you get out of the water. That way your beach towel, that you might want to sprawl on, isn't soaking wet. Being frugal, I bought a knock off at my favorite dollar store.

Corral the Laundry

A pop up laundry hamper takes up minimal space in the suitcase,   keeps dirty clothes together, and fits nicely in a corner of the cabin's closet. Dirty clothes can be simply stuffed into a suitcase, hamper and all, on the way home. Discount stores sell them for $4; mine came from the dollar store. It's lasted at least a dozen cruises so far.

OR

Bring along a large trash bag. Put it into your empty suitcase under the bed when you unpack. Throw dirty/worn clothes into it at the end of the day. By the time the cruise is over, almost all your packing is already done. Tie up the laundry bag, toss it into your suitcase, and stuff shoes around it. Done! I'm a big fan of simplifying.

Let the bathroom be your steamer - hang wrinkled clothes on hangers in the bathroom while you enjoy a hot, steamy shower with the door closed. Those wrinkles will disappear in a hurry.

Dining with a baby or toddler? Those bibs will be disgusting by the end of the cruise! Rather than bringing your own, use a cloth napkin and a safety pin. Leave it on the table after the meal. They're going to do laundry anyway. Or, you could buy disposable bibs for use on the ship.

Tucking a fabric softener sheet in your luggage helps keep clothing fresher. It's seriously nasty to open a suitcase full of last-week's laundry at home.

My method for clean vs. nearly-clean tops: if I wear a shirt for just a short time, and don't spill anything on it, it can be worn again, but it's not as clean as an unworn item. As a reminder, it goes back on a hanger, but inside out. Pants can be worn at least a couple of times, unless my soup jumps off the spoon. At home, all inside out clothing is automatically relegated to the laundry hamper, while right-side –out clothing is still clean, and goes back in the closet. Make up your own system if you prefer---I'll never know.

Ship's Laundry Service

You can send out your clothes to the **ship's laundry**. It takes about 24-36 hours. The **advantage** to this is that you get fresh undies, and your clothes are returned in a little basket, neatly folded, with tissue paper, which probably does not happen at home. Prices are for all you can fit in the bag, not individual items. Clean clothes take up less room than wadded up dirty ones, which can help with packing. The **disadvantage**s: not all items are included; often, dresses, blouses, jeans, slacks, and jackets are not washed.   Isn't that what I needed to be cleaned? Clothes are dried on high heat, and that can shrink your tee shirts faster than a third   trip to the buffet dessert bar. You clothes will be tagged with little stickers, and washed together with everyone else's.

The ship's laundry charge is by the bag, not the item, so you need to **get as much in the bag as possible** to make it more cost effective. Roll, not cram, your clothes into the bag provided, and reinforce with tape to get the most items in the deal. It's okay to slightly overflow, so long as your undies don't fall out when the cabin steward takes the bag to the laundry service.

If you choose to use the ship's laundry, **wait for about the fourth day of the cruise,** when there will be a price break offered.

What to Pack and Not Pack

What to Bring?

A sense of humor, and some patience, along with the ability to adjust plans due to the unexpected on your vacation is the best thing you can pack. Whatever happens is hardly ever dire, and certainly not worth getting your blood pressure all up in the stratosphere. **Expect things to be different than home.** That's why you left, isn't it?

I plan by thinking about **what each day will require.** For example, a port day might include: a swim, followed by a hike with a chilly cave in the middle, shopping at a market, then back on ship, and a formal night for dinner. I'd be sure I had a swimsuit, cover-up, beach shoes, hiking clothes, walking shoes, a warm layer for the cave, a tote for purchases, and nice clothes for dinner. Add in some underclothes, and a comb, and that day's handled.

I taught my kids to pack on their own and at a very young age. Before they could read, I'd draw little pictures of what to pack! Self-reliance is a good skill. Besides, I was outnumbered.

My good friend packs for any cruise a minimum of *two weeks* ahead of time. This, in my opinion, is ridiculous! Besides taking a serious dent in her wardrobe, all of her packed items get very wrinkled. I tend to pack the morning we leave, or the day before if we have an early flight. I do have a list, so it's just a matter of assembling everything. You make your own way.

Check the weather reports before you leave so you can be prepared. This way you can pack the correct things, and not complain that Glacier Bay is too cold, or Barbados too hot for what you packed!

I'd rather have what I want and not need it, then to need it and not have it. However, **cruises are quite civilized**, so pack reasonably. It's not a camping trip.

A Packing List

A packing list ---in some form—is essential. Otherwise, you're liable to show up for your cruise without any shirts, or underwear, or something else you consider important. I'm not going to bore you with endless packing lists.

Online Lists abound. If your personality demands a detailed inventory, there are loads of packing lists online. Do a search for "Packing List Cruise" and dozens will pop up. Good luck-- you'd need a couple of steamer trunks and two Sherpa to haul it all!

 Following are a few things I consider essential, besides the usual clothing, toiletries, and comfy shoes.

I bring a small pharmacy, because scouting out a band aid on a ship is a chore, and if I need anything stronger, the medical staff can get all up in arms. My supply fits nicely in a large zip lock bag. School pencil boxes also work well, but don't squish as well as a bag.

Our first aid type box includes:

 prescription medicines (enough for a week longer than planned; you never know)

over-the-counter items to treat sniffles: decongestants, throat lozenges band aids, small gauze, disinfectant wipes ---it's easier to get a tiny first aid kit

super glue for paper cuts

anti-itch creme for bug bites --- Gold Bond is the best I've found for itches!

antacids, Pepto , Imodium, Tums

anti-inflammatory medicine, such as Tylenol, plus headache pills

Benadryl (new places can trigger allergies you didn't know you had)

100% aloe, for sunburn, rashes, chafing

triple anti biotic creme

a sharp thin needle for splinter extraction

orajel or clove oil, for sudden tooth aches

moleskin for hot spots that will turn into a blister if not thwarted

cotton swabs and a few cotton balls

emery boards   (a jagged nail can make you nuts!)

Being Prepared Is Not Just For Boy Scouts!

Other items I always pack include:

batteries/chargers for the camera, cell phone, e-readers

cell phone

a few large safety pins for wardrobe malfunctions. Duct tape is great to hitch up a sagging hem

small safety pins

small sewing kit (or a few lengths of thread wrapped around a cardboard, with a needle)

reading glasses (several pair; mine migrate)

disinfectant cleaning wipes (we swipe the cabin's hard surfaces first thing)

travel-size hand sanitizer, or two

packaged snacks; hard candy, granola bars, dried fruit (mostly for shore days)

playing cards (and travel-size games for longer cruises with extra sea days)

sunglasses -- bring two; one usually gets sat upon

child-size scissors (to remove those pesky little plastic tags on purchases) lip balm   is crucial. Ocean breezes are delightful, but can chap your lips before you know it

eye drops (same reason)

a travel size bottle of hand sanitizer, travel size Kleenex and hand wipes for the port-day bag. Not all bathrooms on shore are wonderful, and every time I've tried to use a biffy behind a tree in some wild place, I invariably fill my shoe.

sunscreen

What Else to Pack?

Make sure your sunscreen is fresh; it expires after a year. Our daughter got severe sunburn on St Maarten, although we carefully reapplied the sunblock throughout the day. Last year's tube from the closet was a bad idea. Aloe saved her.

Mosquito repellent can be a godsend. Who would believe we'd be eaten alive in Alaska? Mosquitos are the state bird, and they can be intense. Our daughter complained the darned things got between her binoculars and her eyeballs more than once. The ruins in South America are also guarded by aggressive bugs. I've heard a fabric softener sheet tucked in a pocket repels the nasty biters, but I never seem to remember to pack any.

Swimmer's ear can be so painful! You should pick up some ear-drying medicine at a drugstore at home, if you and your head plan on being underwater much.

Guest Services desk has earplugs (handy for snoring cabin mates), along with headache pills, safety pins, seasick remedies, playing cards, razors, pens, toothbrushes, scratch paper, mending kit, etc, just for the asking. Don't make a pest of yourself.

In an emergency, a **tiny powerful flashlight could be a lifesaver**, or at least a morale booster. The chances of a full blown crisis are very slim, but so is my flashlight, and it makes me feel better!

If you wear glasses, take an extra pair! Husband (alias The Cruise Addict) lost his when a wave took them off his face at Orient Beach. I was able to spot them under the clear water, and quickly retrieved them, but it could have been bad. There's always a risk of sitting on the glasses, or dropping them over the railing, or worse--- just bring extra!

Toiletries

Pack **liquid toiletries** (shampoo, etc) in quart bags to contain explosions in the suitcase. Same concept on beach days; I dislike sunscreen on my magazine, so they are kept separate.

Basic toiletries are available onboard, but they are very expensive. $16 is high for a bottle of contact lens solution, and it's not even your favorite brand. If you can't bring your favorite liquids from home, allow time to stop in Walmart, CVS, etc, near the embarkation port to get necessities.

Don't bring brand-new or full sized toiletries on a cruise. They take up too much space, and you're not really going to use 8oz of toothpaste in seven days, are you? Better to bring a nearly-empty one, then throw it away when you're done. Travel sized items are everywhere. Or, make your own. Buy empty travel sized bottles, and fill them with your own shampoo, conditioner, or whatever you like. Be sure to label them; white liquids are white liquids.

If you do buy new bottles of anything, even travel sized bottles, and you're flying to the port, **use a little first at home**. Plastic bottles and their contents expand at high altitudes, and can make a mess in your suitcase. Yet another reason to pack liquids in bags.

While you're at it, **bring your favorite soap, or body wash, if you have a preference**. I trusted the cruise line's touted fabulous body washes, because I'm generally not fussy. Yuck. It made me feel waxy, as if I could not get it off of me! I asked everyone in sight for a bar of soap, even tried to buy some in the sundry shop. Every crew member launched into a spiel about the wonderful body wash, but offered no soap. I was miserable. That particular cruise began with three sea days, which is a very long time to feel waxed into one's own skin. First stop in first port: a store to buy a decent bar of ordinary soap. Ahh!

Shipboard hairdryers can be wimpy. If you don't favor the look of seriously windswept hair, consider packing your own.

You might pack your own **hair care products** as well. Never quite sure what's in those dinky bottles the cabin steward leaves for you. Worse, the mystery goo in the wall dispensers.

Is That Everything? (almost)

Take your driver's license with you, just in case you decide at the last minute to rent a vehicle while in a port. Those little scooters are tempting.

I always take **the shower caps** left in hotels, and stuff them in tote bag corners, out of the way. In a sudden rain storm, these make instant camera covers.

I pack an **extra tote bag**, the kind that folds flat. It takes up almost no room, and is it handy! It's good for shore days, taking a change of clothes to the gym, walking around town so you have a place to put your purchases, and doubles as another carry- on on the way home if you buy too much stuff. That can happen.

Large plastic trash bags can be handy for dirty laundry for the trip home. Some organized folks even have two for laundry, and sort it as they undress. At home, each bag is a washer load, already sorted by color.

Large trash bags can also be used to line the inside of your luggage if your embarkation port is having a monsoon. A bag is cheap insurance to keep your belongings waterproof if it looks like your luggage might be left in rain or snow.

Bring ear plugs if you're a light sleeper. It'll help block out the folks who forget how much voices travel down the hall at 3 am. it'll also avoid unpleasantness, such as that time when I awoke to find our daughter, quietly chucking rolled up washcloths at her snoring father.

Super glue can be the most useful thing you pack, but is not to be found onboard. I know this because I once broke a toenail very short, and went on a hunt to buy or borrow some glue to fill it in. It hurt with every step, until I could reach a drugstore in port the following day! Super glue is also a handy thing to repair a necklace clasp, or to hold your glasses together once that tiny screw falls out.

I like to know what time it is---I wear a watch about as often as I wear fingernails---so I set a **small travel alarm clock in** the cabin. You can get wake up calls on every ship, but that's just not what I need when I wake up and it's dark and what time is it anyway? 3 am and 3 pm look a lot alike in a dark cabin!

I always pack an **empty spray bottle**, a plastic plant mister. Filled with tap water, I can use it to encourage wrinkles to fall out of clothing, cool off a sunburned back, remove that sticky spot where someone set their soda down, and even fluff up my curls. My hair looks best in humid conditions. A spritz of water can save a whole styling.

Tuck a deck of playing cards in your carry-on bag. You never know when you'll be stuck in a line somewhere, and cards trump whining from boredom, so to speak.

Contraband

There are certain **items you cannot bring onboard a cruise ship**. Most have to do with potential for fires, or power drain, or passenger safety. Fire is the biggest hazard onboard ---as you'll learn at every muster drill—and since ships create their own electricity, they're conscious of not squandering it.

 What can't you bring onboard? Irons, candles, lighters, weapons and explosives are the biggies. Appliances are also banned, so don't pack your toaster, coffeemaker, or hotplate. Some ships ban those long power strips, the kind with a row of outlets, but allow the little ones with 3 outlets and no cord. Extension cords are often banned as well. Policy on alcohol varies by cruise line; some ban it all, others allow a specified amount.

There's some confusion now that a few US states permit **marijuana** use. Even if that is true in your home state, you can still be in trouble if the cruise line or port police find drugs in your luggage, your cabin, or on your person. In many ports, those sniffer dogs check out the ship while passengers are off playing. It's a sure way to spoil your trip, so don't say I didn't warn you.

Quite a few passengers have had **extension cords** confiscated upon boarding, but if you need one, you can borrow one on the ship.

Packing Tips

Cross packing

Many cruisers swear by **cross packing**. Whomever you travel with, pack half of your things in each other's luggage. That way, if one suitcase gets lost at least you still have some clothes. I admit this does not fit my style. Husband (alias The Cruise Addict) has a very different packing style than mine, not to mention his clothes are quite a bit larger than mine. The first time we tried cross packing, it made me a little crazy. Okay, that was also the last time, now that I think about it. I compromise; I pack one extra outfit in my carryon, which does not leave my arm until we reach the cabin. Oh, and I cross my fingers, which is almost like cross-packing, right?

You can buy **fancy space-saver packing bags**, but did I mention I'm cheap? I buy **large clear plastic zip lock bags, gallon size or bigger.** Sometimes you can even find jumbo size. I neatly fold my clothes, slip a stack into the bag, then flatten it. I use my behind or lie on my front to squish out most of the air as I seal the bag. It saves so much space that packing overweight bags can be an issue. Be careful about potential audiences. You want to be sure no one is taking pictures of you laid out flat, sucking air out of a bag while you're packing. Don't ask me why.

I always use the above method for my unmentionables, at least, since The Incident. I was flying to my mother's surprise birthday party. My siblings had designated me as the party-decorations getter, the sillier the better. I had just a carry-on, with clothes for the weekend, the decorations, and a two pound block of Mom's favorite local sharp cheddar cheese. The TSA people at the airport went a little nuts; lights flashing, people running, and suddenly my bag was upended and contents strewn down a thirty foot conveyor belt, streamers, banners, undies, and all. How was I supposed to know **sharp Cheddar has the same density as C-4 explosives**?

Preventing Wrinkles (in clothing, not faces)

Layer thin dry cleaning plastic between layers of clothing as you pack your suitcase. The slippery surface prevents wrinkles when slipped between shirts, blouses, slacks, jackets, etc. You can substitute tissue paper if you have it at hand. Just fold it right in with the clothing. Everything comes out wrinkle free and ready to wear.

If this fails, we hang wrinkled items on a hanger when we unpack, and **spray them lightly with a plant mister full of tap water**. By the time they dry, wrinkles have vanished. Why is it always Husband's shirts that get so wrinkled?

 I had a friend who ironed her husband's shirt every night before dinner on the cruise. I told her to stay away from my Husband (alias The Cruise Addict); she's obviously not a good influence! If you're old enough to be a husband, you're certainly old enough to care for your own shirts.

Obviously, items left wadded in suitcases for longer periods wrinkle more than ones unpacked at first opportunity. For us, **unpacking is just a first day chore.**

Children's play clothes seldom wrinkle, and that's what they wear on cruises. Plan ahead to get your little one dressed in a hurry, while encouraging independence. As you pack, **place a day's clothing in a single large zip lock bag**. Shorts, shirt, socks,

underwear, all in one spot. Hand the kid the bag labeled
Tuesday; tell them to put on everything in the bag. You can then
turn your attention to other things, while the child gets the
satisfaction of dressing All By Myself. You know that's
important.

I pack **a few thin wire hangers,** the dry cleaner type. Yes, I know
they will bring extras if asked, but we've had several cruises
where the cabin steward said they had run out, or only gave us
2-3, and even when they do bring them, it's often after I've
unpacked. Mine take up very little room.

More Packing

TSA forbids locking your suitcases properly, but those pesky zippers can slide open. I **thread a wire twisty off a bread wrapper through the zipper tabs** after I pack. The zipper will stay closed, but TSA can inspect if they get a notion. Why is it always *my* suitcase they choose to rifle through?

To cut down on overweight bags at the airport, **put your heavier items into your carryon bags,** especially shoes, sneakers, electronics and books.

After your cruise, as you unpack, **make a quick list of what clothing you actually wore** and what you did not need after all. Put this list into your empty suitcase when you sort it. It'll help avoid bringing clothes you never had on on your next cruise, or at least give you a good starting point in packing.

Wear the heavy and/or bulky stuff on the plane; your biggest shoes, sweaters, and jackets. Once on board, take what you don't need off, and use it as a pillow, or stuff it in the bins or the under the seat in front of you.

Unpacking Onboard

Take time to **unpack and organize your stuff**. That's just a required first-day chore, like attending the muster drill. Working as a team, Husband (alias The Cruise Addict) and I can unpack in 10 minutes flat. Putting your clothes away prevent wrinkles, and makes the rest of the week easier. Trust me, you'll appreciate it in the long run.

Some passengers pack their **clothes still on the hangers.** Once onboard, they hang the clothes, hangers and all, right in the closet. I find this takes up precious suitcase room, but it may work better for you.

I double up **clothes on the hangers** in the closet, to save space, as I unpack. I've also had good luck with closet space savers. They have 5-6 holes you can loop a wire hanger though horizontally, and then they fall vertically on the closet rod. You can fit several outfits in the space one hanger would have taken up.

Don't Forget

The Virtues of Zip Lock Bags

I always always always! pack a wad of **different sized zip lock bags**. The snack size is good for tiny things, like earrings and coins. Sandwich size is just right for a pretty rock or some souvenir sand. Don't take any of it from Hawaii. It's Pele's and she doesn't share well. Research stories of Pele's wrath if you don't believe me. Jumbo bags are great for keeping damp or smelly clothes separated from dry things on the way home, as well as wet swimsuits if you took a dip after dinner the last night of the cruise.

Sandwich bags make decent ice packs for sore knees from too much dancing.

Zip-lock baggies, preferably the thicker freezer-type, are great for keeping things dry, especially when you go to the beach. You can stuff your credit cards, driver's licenses, cash, etc. in them and keep them safe inside your bathing suit. Pressing air out prevents extra bulges. I recommend double-bagging them and you won't have any problems with leakage. I actually prefer these to the expensive dive bag we bought. We were surprised to see cash floating by on the waves not a minute after the dive bag filled with water and set the contents free!

I find more uses every time we cruise!

Office supplies fit in another little zip lock bag. It contains a little scissor, clear tape, super glue, post it notes, a pen, highlighter, safety pins, paper clips, rubber bands, 2-3 clothespins, a few 3X5 cards, and an emery board. Takes up very little room, and you'd be amazed at how often we reach for this bag!

What to Wear?

A very common cruise tip is as follows: **Don't bring so many clothes;** nobody cares if you wear the same thing twice. Disregard this tip if you are the type who tends to spill soup or ketchup on every shirt you own.

I seldom stain my clothing, but I **disregard the above tip**. I *could* pack less... you'll read about people who do a four week cruise with just a backpack and a large purse, or those who wear the same blue pants and black top for a week, jazzing it up with different scarves---as if that helps! I do pack mix-and-match items, **making sure each item can be worn at least three ways.** However, I crave variety and color, so I technically over pack. For a seven day cruise, I'll likely bring ten tops. I often change several times a day at home, too. There's always a chance that I will not be able to stand looking at the same black blouse One. More. Time. So long as I don't ask you to carry my suitcase, you don't get a vote.

Pack layers for cold weather They are less bulky than the 1940's style parka, and you can peel off shirts and sweaters as you warm up.

Silk long underwear is a wonderful invention. It's light weight, comfortable, and truly works. You can't enjoy the day if you're freezing.

The best thing to wear on a cruise ship is layers. Even if it's a hot, sunny day, it can be windy on deck, the air conditioning in the dining rooms tends to be brisk, crowded corridors get warm fast... you could be changing clothes all day long. I wear wraps or pashminas on the ship. They're light, but block the draft from a vent as needed. They're also pretty!

Take a light-weight sweater, wrap, or a windbreaker (or just a long-sleeve blouse). Or, decide ahead of time to buy one of the ubiquitous wraps they sell onboard for $10. It's a nice reminder of your cruise.

A pretty **sarong can be the most useful item you take**! It can be folded and tied into a skirt, halter top, vest, dress, shawl, swimsuit cover-up, even as a bag in a pinch. Sarongs are also great for improvising a changing curtain, beach blanket, or nursing cover, but the best use is to block chilly breezes from an aggressive air conditioning vent. If you forgot sunblock, and get sunburned, a sarong is the softest item of clothing you own. Google "how to tie a sarong" for ideas.

Shoes

Wrap your shoes in plastic grocery bags to prevent sole soil from getting on your clothing in your suitcase. Another plastic bag is always useful!

High heels are for land-lubbers! Go with some comfortable flats or wedges when the ship is moving. You don't need a twisted ankle due to a rolling ship to ruin your cruise. Even the professional dancers switch to flats when the ship is rocking. They do; notice next time!

Bring good walking shoes. Trust me - those heels might be cute, but after sixteen trips from one end of the ship to the other - you will be happy you listened to me.

Binoculars

Bring your own binoculars. There are amazing things to see, especially where the ship isn't far from land. You don't want to be the one begging for a glimpse of whales breaching or oil derricks nearby, when no one wants to share their binoculars.

Opera glasses work well, often weigh less than binoculars, slip into a pocket, and don't even need adjusting.

Binoculars are as useful indoors as outdoors. They can bring details into clearer focus in museums, cathedrals, and other buildings to examine the artwork, sculptures, and architectural elements.

Duct Tape to the Rescue!

Duct tape is versatile and comes in 27 pretty colors! Duct tape can:

hold up a **ripped-out hem**,

secure your **tote bag handle** ,

reinforce the **paper laundry bag** for ship's laundry service,

prevent a **blister**,

hold a **broken flip flop** together,

repair a **suitcase** mauled in transit,

remove **lint** from an outfit,

hold a curtain closed so you can sleep in,

repair a **camera case,**

Prevent your **film** from rolling out of your case,

cover a **hole in your tote bag,**

childproof a cabinet or drawers

remove a splinter from your hand,

or **a tick** from your leg,

hold a shoe together until it can be fixed or replaced,

improvise   **a Band-Aid** or even a sling

secure **prescription bottles** from rattling around in a case,

double seal a liquid **toiletry bottle** in transit

you can wrap a strip all the way around your **suitcase** for added security,

and fashion a **waterproof folder** for papers

or even a slim **wallet** for port days

A strip of bright duct tape across the back of your child's shirt could make the kids **more visible on a playground** in port.

A strip of the silver kind inside your shoe provides **extra insulation** in snow; the silver reflects heat back onto your foot.

Our **balcony door slammed** over and over in the wind, and I wished I had remembered to bring a strip of duct tape to hold it closed. Probably a bad idea anyway...duct tape can leave a sticky residue. But in an emergency, any port in the storm, as they say!

A roll of duct tape is pretty bulky. You can easily **pack a few strips,** torn off and stuck on the inside of one of your suit cases. Flat, out of the way, and right at hand!

Another idea is to **wrap a strip or two of duct tape around a stiff cardboard**, cut about credit-card size. Packs flat, and it's ready to peel off at a moment's notice. Or **around a permanent marker**—you'll need one for notes, anyway.

Shopping and Shipping

If you can, **postpone shopping on the ship the first few days**. The sales in the shops and at the spa come on strong as you get closer to the end of the cruise. Yes, I know you are tempted, but a bargain's worth the wait, isn't it?

Read ahead of time to know what you **cannot bring home,** or back onboard; fresh fruits, meats, dairy items are risky.

Souvenirs

Ask crew members where to get souvenirs; they know. They are working, but they have family at home, too.

Want to bring home souvenirs without breaking the bank? Consider visiting a grocery store or market in your destination ports to buy that special chocolate, olive oil, local candy, fancy vanilla, vinegar, spices, or whatever else the place is known for.

Don't be a snob; some of my favorite finds have come from swap meets, local markets, and street fairs. They come with a story, too!

You know **you can keep your key card,** right? It's a memento of your cruise, right in your hand. It has the ship's name, your name, even the date. Husband still bemoans the fact that not all of his early key cards were preserved. How was I supposed to know he'd become The Cruise Addict? I thought we were just on a vacation!

A fairly inexpensive memento is local coins and small paper currency. Interesting, easy to find, small to pack, and you never know when your kids might need that very coin for a social studies project. Obviously, this works better in foreign ports.

A common tourist purchase in the Bahamas and some Caribbean islands is straw goods. Hats, bags, fans, toys, all cleverly woven of local straw or palm fronds, for very low prices. Admire all you want, even purchase a broad-brimmed hat for your day at the beach, but be aware that straw **items are almost never allowed back on ships**. They carry tiny mites, which could cause havoc with the ship's mini ecosystem. Eeeww... mites on my head at the beach...I'll take the sunburned face, please!

If you are on **a quest for a particular item**, only locals know where to begin your hunt. That special yarn, the caribou horn buttons, a lobster-shaped cookie cutter, local syrups and teas, regional calendars and cookbooks; these things are just not listed in guidebooks. These make great souvenirs. How many tacky tee shirts do you need?

The crew, including the cabin stewards, waiters, and entertainment staff, are probably your **best source of information** regarding advice on areas in ports to seek or stay away from. Think about it—they've been there over and over!

 Most people cruise during the high season, right in the middle of the ship's prime time in that area. Shopping deals are to be had at the *end* of that period, as merchants realize **this is their last chance to sell out their wares**. Consider, for example, how Alaska works.

Alaska's southwest coast is a huge cruise ship region. They sell so much stuff to tourists that the towns have to import clerks and cashiers from the Lower 48 to man their shops! At the end of the summer, these towns pretty much fold up, and resume their sleepy, passenger-less identities. **The last couple of cruises of the season promise prices of 75-90%** off the very things people paid full price for last week!

I'm not saying you should plan a cruise around end-of-season shopping bargains, exactly. Well. Maybe a little.

Shipping Items Home

If your cruise has a USA port, and you over shopped, think about stopping at a post office to **mail home some flat-rate boxes.** They're often cheaper than the airlines' overweight luggage fees. The cutoff point is two pounds. If the contents weigh more than that, flat rate is the way to go; for less, use a regular box. The rule is, if it fits in the box, it costs the flat rate, whether you mail rocks or feathers. In Hawaii, our daughter wanted to stock up on a little glutinous rice, which is apparently not available on the mainland. About 40 lbs of the stuff. Yes, the postal clerk had an odd expression, but she also complimented us on avoiding the airline fees. This is a great tip if you buy that marble nativity set. You're on your own if you buy the seven foot tall giraffe.

Telling Time in Ports

Read your daily ship schedule for details about getting on and off the ship in ports. Times in the port will be clearly laid out, including what time to be back onboard. All will list the ship's contact information, needed in case you have a major problem, or miss the ship. The paper will tell you how to use a tender, if the port's dock is too small or unavailable. Most importantly, it will tell you what you must take off the ship.

All cruise lines require your key card/sea pass card coming and going. Some ports also require a photo ID for anyone over the age of sixteen. Depending on how foreign your port is, a driver's license or passport is ideal.

It's important to know which clock to follow, as some ships use ship's time, while others go by local time. Mildly confusing, but did you know that the Japanese Navy still goes by Japan time, regardless of where they are in the world? 2 am could be lunchtime!

Watch your watch in port. We always double check the time to be back on the ship, and aim to be back onboard about 45 minutes before we absolutely have to. The ship <u>will</u> leave on time, with or without you. Have you seen those YouTube videos of people running frantically down the dock, screaming at the ship as it pulls away? Don't be those people.

We have cut it close a few times. There was that time in Juneau, Alaska. Our family had taken a shuttle out to Mendenhall Glacier, and it was a lovely day for a hike to the waterfall, as the ranger suggested. Our son ran ahead....about a mile ahead, past the waterfall, all the way to the top of the trail. Our cell phones did not have service, so we had no way to remind him the ship would leave in under an hour, and we still had to hike back, and then catch a shuttle to the ship. Husband (alias The Cruise Addict) was increasingly frantic, as we realized the odds of us missing the ship were pretty high. He gets like that. At last our son ran back, we rushed to catch the next shuttle, and we boarded the ship with a good six minutes to spare. Son had some great photos of an old gold mine train he had found way up the trail. Husband (alias The Cruise Addict)'s blood pressure was too astronomical to appreciate them for a while.

Oh, there was the other time, in Antigua... we had an all-day private tour, and it ended 40 minutes before the ship was to sail. Wait! I was in the Spice Islands! and I had not had time to buy any spices. We asked our driver to drop us off at the market where locals shop. He told us dubiously we did not have time, since the ship was about a 25 minute walk from the market. He underestimated my shopping skills. I broke a land speed record for spice –seeking. I filled a bag with aromatic cinnamon, nutmeg with mace still attached, vanilla, allspice, dried herbs and seeds, essences of things I'd only read about, and we ran. True, the crew was disassembling the gangway as we sprinted to the ship, but we made it. Barely.

A tip here: **if you miss the ship, you're on your own.** You'll have to make your way to the next port of call to catch up, at your own expense. The exception is if you are on a ship-sponsored shore excursion. If the ships leaves while you're on a ship-sponsored tour, the cruise line will fly you to the next port. Perhaps the peace of mind is worth being herded like sheep onto crowded buses, if you're a really fearful traveler. If you are even slightly brave, or can operate a clock, you're much better off the beaten path.

They Know More Than You Do

Ask a Local

We make a point of asking local residents for advice on where to go and what not to miss. Really, who knows their hometown better than they do? A simple question may net you the best whale watching spot, an interesting place to see a local product being made, a unique shop, a tasty hole-in-the-wall restaurant for lunch, or a pristine uncrowded beach. Ask!

I've even heard of local people offering to drive tourists to the sights themselves. If you're that lucky, you owe them lunch. At least!

Locals can also offer advice on alternative ways to travel, such as a ferry that goes to the same island as the expensive tour boat (and has fewer rowdy drunks), public transportation, private tours, etc. We're not familiar with subways, and were baffled by Boston's T. After a 45 second consultation with a woman walking by, we were experts, riding it confidently all over the city.

In San Francisco, a local guy told us to walk up one block to catch the Cable Cars, to avoid the long wait at the terminus. Husband (alias The Cruise Addict) disregarded his advice...but we *could* have skipped a long wait! Listening to advice offered by those who know is also a good tip.

(In my defense, you can't get a ticket for the cable cars one block up; we'd have had to purchase it on the cable car itself---The Cruise Addict.)

(so what?—Author)

Some of our most enjoyable activities on shore have been non-touristy ones. We seek local flavor, off the beaten path. **I like Visitor's Centers and National and State Parks.** One of our fun memories is of a 45 minute walking tour in Skagway, with a National Park Ranger. She was a story teller, and we laughed as we soaked up history and colorful stories. Cost? Free!

A Visitor's Center is a compact introduction to the area. **Local museums** are also worthwhile. My head is chock full of facts you'll never know, because I seek out quirky local places that most people walk on by. You may never get back there—be where you are and soak it up while you can!

I Don't Feel So Good

Norovirus, And Swollen Ankles

You've heard of **norovirus**, and probably think it's a cruise ship disease. It's not; it shows up in groups of people, such as schools, nursing homes, sporting events, everywhere. Last year it sickened a whole cheerleading camp. I've read that 80% of cases of "stomach flu" or gastroenteritis are actually norovirus.

 The most effective way to prevent the spread of norovirus is by washing your hands...a lot, like every time you're within ten feet of soap and water. The anti-bacterial hand sanitizer that's everywhere on ships has no effect on viruses, but use it anyway. It's a backup for other germs.

You'll see cruise crew members cleaning all over the ship, but they just can't be everywhere at once. I'm careful not to touch surfaces that many other people touch. I **press elevator buttons with a knuckle, and lightly graze railings with an elbow on stairs for stability**. Husband (alias The Cruise Addict) teases me for being cautious, but so far, I've been lucky.

Another precaution we take is to quickly wipe every hard surface of the cabin, especially knobs and handles and light switches and the remote control with t**he disinfectant wipes** that I brought from home. It's just part of our routine on Day One. Why should a previous passenger's grubby hands ruin <u>my</u> trip?

Swollen ankles? Cruise ship foods, like most restaurant meals, tend to have a lot of salt in them. It's likely more salt than you use at home, and it can cause your ankles and hands to swell. Other than leaving your already-tight shoes at home, there are a few things you can try to sidestep pain. Avoid obviously   salty foods: bacon, sausage, cheeses, cold cuts, pickled items. Non-fruit soups and sauces contain a surprising amount of salt.

Drink plenty of water to flush the salt out of your system. Eating a lot of raw **fruits and vegetables** offsets the salt. Oats, celery, tomatoes, cantaloupe, watermelon, honeydew, spinach and   parsley are all natural diuretics, and all are right there handy at any buffet.

If the swelling gets bad, try a figure-eight elastic bandage wrap on your ankles at night, or elevate your feet with a rolled towel.

Seasickness

Why Do I Feel This Awful?

Seasickness, or any motion sickness, is caused when what your eyes see doesn't match what your body is feeling. It can be triggered by one of two things: either your body feels motion that your eyes can't see, or your eyes see motion your body cannot feel.

When you are below decks on a ship, everything in the room looks stationary to your eyes, but your body can feel the ship's motion. Your mind expects you to be able to stand perfectly still, but your body's reaction to the movement you feel contradicts this expectation.

The second form of disconnect occurs when your body is either still, or moving steadily enough that your inner ears can compensate for the motion, but your eyes perceive more motion than there actually is. This can happen during the action scene of a movie on a big screen, or even fast-paced dancers on a ship's stage, if you're sitting in the back of the theatre.

More to the Point, Make It Stop!

The reality is that **less than three percent of passengers become seasick**, but if you're one of them, you won't care about statistics.

Many people recommend wearing those behind-the-ear patches prescribed by doctors; others curse the side effects. Sea bands, that put pressure on a wrist tendon, are surprisingly effective with no side effects. Queasy Beads do the same thing, and look more stylish.

Booking a cabin midships is best, if you tend towards seasickness.

Hold a pencil horizontally by the middle. Wiggle it. See how both ends move more than the center? Ships are like that. In wild water, that can make the difference between the motion of the ocean being a pleasant thing, or more than you can handle.

Lower decks have less access to fresh air, but also less movement in a storm.

Popular seasickness remedies include eating green apple, or fresh pear. Eating anything with real ginger in it, tea or candied, or even ginger ale or ginger snaps, can help. Some cruise lines hand out candied ginger in rough seas. Sucking on green olives, sipping lemon lime soda, and eating enough to prevent your stomach from going all-out empty also reduces the queasy sensation.

Bonine is a common remedy, as is sucking on a cut lemon or strong lemon candy.

A cabin steward suggested peeling **an orange**, holding the rind to the nose, and inhaling. It can't hurt.

 Go out on deck. Looking at the horizon will remind your brain that you are still on earth, and the fresh air will do you good.

Peppermint, ginger tea, or crystalized ginger all ease seasickness, taken early and often. Sometimes just sucking on a hard candy will head off symptoms, as will sipping water.

Sea Legs and Stabilizers

Most of today's **cruise ships are so big that you won't feel any extreme ocean motion**—and probably won't get seasick. Most have stabilizers, little fins that jut out of the sides of the ship under the waterline to hold it steadier in rough waters. However, use of stabilizers cost a lot to use, so the Captain may not choose to use them as often or as soon as you'd like.

Ever heard of someone getting their "sea legs"? When you first notice significant motion of the ship, go out on deck and walk around for a little while. It helps your inner ear accept the fact that you are now at sea, not on a sidewalk, and can head off motion sickness.

If you do start to feel queasy, avoid doing anything "little," such as reading, needlework, flower arranging, card playing, or examining your breakfast in too much detail.   One night our teen aged son oozed into our cabin, an unhealthy shade of green. The ship was rocking, so I had warned him not to read. He moaned, "I didn't! I was stringing beads in the teen club. Ginger, please!" He knew better.

I personally don't get seasick, not even in that relentless storm that lasted twenty-two hours, not even that night when I woke up to a weird gurgling sound, which turned out to be water sloshing out of the toilet, whitecaps and everything. The Captain said waves were 13-18 meters high. Even so, I just don't get seasick.   Our daughter in law does, though, and with enthusiasm. She suffered and moaned all *day long*. She finally took some free pills given out by the Guest Service desk. I don't know what they were, but they had a miraculous effect. Within 20 minutes, she was in the mood for a chili cheese dog.

That made me feel sick.

Listen to Your Kids

On a related topic, remember **that children can also get seasick**. Their first symptom is often a headache. You want to take children's complaints seriously. Trust me on this. During that same twenty-two- hour long storm off the Pacific coast, we had our small granddaughter with us, while her aforementioned mother was dying of seasickness, or fearing she would live after all. Feeling fine, we went along with the plan for the day, with child in tow. She did mention her head hurt, but ...well, kids grumble.

Our first inkling she was sincere was as we were playing a game in the observation lounge at the end of the ship. She mentioned "I'm going to throw up, *right now*" and darned if she didn't follow through, right on the carpet. She bounced back quickly, almost as quickly as the crew cleaned it up. She is a naturally cheerful little soul, and did not complain, although she also tossed her cookies twice more that day.

Worst though, was when she decided she was hungry. We chose the aft dining room for a late lunch. Very back of the ship; slow learners, I guess. We all ordered, then a stricken expression crossed the child's face. Uh,oh. I grabbed her arm and raced her across the dining room to the restroom. She barfed in the narrow hallway on the way in. She barfed again in the sink, on the floor, in the other sink, in the third sink, and at last made it to the toilet. Shaken, she gasped, "I think I'm all empty." Well, I should think so!

Moral of the story: Take young ones' complaints seriously. And if you're with a sickie, keep her in the middle of the ship, low to the waterline, not in the aft dining room, even if it is nice and empty.

Tummy Trouble and Sunburn

You don't need to pack a whole pharmacy, but do consider **food on the ship is probably richer than you are used to at home.** If you go see the ship's medical staff for tummy issues, they will quarantine you in your cabin for 48 hours. If you are genuinely sick , of course that's best, but if all you needed was some Pepto, Imodium or tums.... you know your guts best.

Sunblock is especially important...a Caribbean cruise can be ruined by a few hours unprotected in the sun! Consider **pure aloe**, in case you fail to apply enough sunblock often enough. **Plain vinegar** is also soothing on sunburned shoulders. Your cabin steward or waiter could obtain some, if you ask nicely.

Food, Food, and More Food

Our friend, John, happily ate everything in sight the first day of his first cruise. He ate two plates of food on his way to dinner, he sampled every dish offered in the buffet, he had three burgers by the pool, he munched six cookies from a platter, he loved the food! He spent the next two days in his cabin, no longer on speaking terms with his digestive system. **Eating lightly is a virtue,** although not one many cruisers aspire to.

Snacks

Pack a few non-perishable snacks. You never know when you'll hit a long line or other delay. That one time in Vancouver comes to mind. Six ships in port, first sailing day of the Alaska season, new staff, and not nearly enough Customs agents led to Disney style lines that reached through three large buildings, and out to the end of the Promenade. We were in line so long, I was worried about people fainting from hunger or from standing that long. We had had a decent breakfast, and planned to lunch on the ship. We didn't get onboard until after dinner time—and we there were still nine hundred passengers on shore when sail away time came (and went). Granola bars or other snacks would have been very welcome!

Cruise food tends to be very good, but sometimes you just **get a craving for something ordinary,** like potatoes chips or a PB&J. The sandwich can be ordered from a children's menu or room service, but you may be out of luck for salty snacks like chips and popcorn. If you tend to crave these, bring a bag along from home, or stop at a store in a port. Even if the onboard gift shop carries these snacks, they'll be very expensive.

Hot Cocoa and Water

Hot cocoa packets are available all day every day at every coffee station, on every ship, along with hot water and cream...except on Glacier Viewing Day in Alaska, when hot cocoa is only available for purchase, for a needlessly high rate. Tip: **stash a few packets the day before**, and mix it with the hot water as needed. Be discreet, because other cruisers may mob you if they see you mixing your own when they just paid $7 for a cup of the same stuff!

Ships purify their own fresh water. Water tastes rather flat by itself. Plan ahead and bring some **Individual packets of lemonade and fruit punch flavors drink mixes** to drop into the water in the stateroom. Crystal Light has a variety of flavors, but off-brands are just as good.

The **drinks and snacks** in your mini-fridge, plus the mineral water in your cabin, are not complimentary, Oh, some are; but only in the more expensive suites. Just avoid them. You're much better off buying a soda at a bar and carrying it to your cabin to drink. It costs that much less!

Passengers can **carry food and drink pretty much everywhere on the ship**, except the spa, workout center, and library. Feel free to take your burger to that lovely window seat, get a plate of veggies to snack on out on deck, or to carry your drink into dinner with you. Cheese and crackers is nice in your cabin. You can also order it from **room service** if you don't mind a short wait.

Main Dining Rooms

Cruise ships prepare food for hundreds of people at each meal, mostly hot, mostly on time. **If you expect five-star food at every meal, you're going to be disappointed.** Preparing thousands of meals a day is more like a banquet service than fine dining. It's unlikely you'll go hungry!

It's nice to ask for a **fruit plate or cheese-and-crackers** while you peruse the menu. If you have the same waiter every night, they'll probably figure it out and have the dish waiting on the table when you sit down.

Another advantage of reading up on your cruise ahead of time is deciding on **dining options**. Most ships have multiple restaurants and choices for dining. Norwegian pioneered Freestyle Dining, and most other lines now have some variation of that. Freestyle and its derivatives let you go to the main dining room any time it's open and sit alone or with whomever you choose, the same as a land-based restaurant.   You can often request a shared table here as well. Both styles have advantages and disadvantages.

On traditional cruise ships, you'll be assigned a specific dinner time and table, with the same people each night. **Dining together is a good way to meet new people.** It's good to get out of your usual comfort zone.

We had a very enjoyable conversation with the environmentally-obsessed couple from inner city Vancouver, although I admit I had never before discussed the food's carbon footprint while looking at a menu. That big burly Texan was interesting, too. I think he forgot to pack a razor; he was scruffier every day. Most people have interesting life stories. You might even learn something.

If your tablemates are **simply too annoying to endure,** however, after you've given them a fair chance, have a word with the Dining Room Manager. They're used to moving people around, and you'll be reseated quickly. This falls into the category of oh-well-we'll-never-see-them-again.

If you have assigned seating dinner, don't be late. It's not polite to keep your table-mates waiting. The waiter will want to serve everyone at the same time; if you're late, you hold up everyone. Of course you are not obliged to show up to the main dining room every night. Specialty restaurants are the big thing on ships. You can also opt for the buffet, room service, or —horrors!-- opt to skip a meal. If you get a moment, it's courteous to let your table-mates or the waiters know, so they don't delay for you. If you find you *are* going to be more than a very few minutes late to an assigned seating, it's best to simply eat somewhere else that night. The dining room is choreography...try not to throw it off.

The first time I cruised, I was a little surprised at the **small portions** served in the dining room. I soon realized that I wasn't used to eating an appetizer, and a salad, and a soup, and bread, and an entrée, and choosing just one dessert was hard. I was in pain during that evening's show**. It's okay to choose just a few things from the menu.** I skip bread, figuring I can always get bread at home. I also often skip breakfast as well. Breakfast is The Cruise Addict's favorite meal, but if I have the choice of facing typical breakfast food or another twenty minutes in bed...bed wins, hands down.

Menus

Main Dining Room dinner menus are posted outside the restaurants after breakfast service is over. Check them to see what appeals to you for dinner that night. If nothing looks good to you, it might be a day to hit the buffet or a specialty restaurant. Or you may spend the afternoon happily anticipating how good the Chicken Cordon Bleu will taste!

Most cruise lines have a menu that rotates weekly, or longer. You may think "Oh, I'll have Chicken Primavera today, and the Scotch Medley tomorrow..." You can't. You'll never see either again in your week long cruise, so decide now! Better yet, order both, or smaller portions of each to try. We often order three entrees for the two of us to share.

Along with the day's offerings, cruise lines have some variation of an **available-every-day menu,** with items such as chicken, steak, salads, pasta. It stays the same all cruise long. I recommend using that page just as a fall back. If none of the daily specials appeal to you, you can always order a steak.

Did you know **adults can order off the children's menu**, and vice versa? Our small granddaughter loves calamari. She was disappointed to see it was not on the children's menu, among the chicken fingers and burgers. She politely ordered three appetizer-sized servings of calamari for dinner off the regular menu, and happily gobbled up every bit, to our waiter's surprise. Sometimes the desserts on the kid menu look more appealing. Brownie sundae, anyone?

Mix It Up---It's Your Dinner

Don't needlessly aggravate the waiters, but **if it's on the menu, feel free to mix it up**. Taste all of the appetizers at one sitting, try two different entrees, ask for three of the desserts if you think you can handle it! You can also order appetizers in entrée size, or entree in appetizer size. Feel free to mix-and-match, so long as it's on the menu somewhere. If the steak has a baked potato and the fish has noodles, you can order fish with baked potato, and no sauce, with extra vegetables.

If you happen to just love the appetizer, **feel free to ask for another** as the waiter returns. It'll be different the following day---now's your chance!

You can order anything off the dining room menu, in any form. Really, you can! They have begun serving smaller portions; reasonable, but less than you're used to seeing in a land-based restaurant. Feel free to order more than one (or two) if you desire---the waiter will not raise an eyebrow. Appetizers are especially small; nothing wrong with ordering three crab cakes. Vegetables are in very small portions; three asparagus spears is not a serving. I always ask for more vegetables at every meal.

One evening we had dinner, but skipped dessert, and during the show, all my sister in law could think of was the Apple Dumpling we had missed. I know that because she kept leaning over to ask, "Do you think it was served warm?" and "I bet it was really flakey" all through the show. As the dancers took their final bow, I whispered, "Would you like to go get an apple dumpling?" Her smile outshone the stage lights. Off we trooped to the main dining room. It was due to close in 25 minutes. I saw the waiter's heart visibly sink as all seven of us were seated in his section...so much for getting off on time! He beamed as we ordered just seven identical desserts, not full meals, and eagerly delivered piping hot, flakey dumplings. Try to be considerate of the crew; they need time off, too.

Now's Your Chance!

Try the chilled soups; they taste like dessert. I'm reminded of that because same sister in law was dubious about the peach berry soup, then ordered an extra bowl for dessert! "Unfamiliar" is not the same as "Bad."

Cruise ships are a great place to **sample unfamiliar and expensive foods**! You don't want to pay $50 for frog's legs or Carpaccio or escargot (and hate it) in a restaurant, but since it doesn't cost any extra on a cruise ship...go for it. You might like it! If you do hate it, ask the waiter to bring you something different. Even if you find a new favorite, enjoy it while you can.

Husband (alias The Cruise Addict) happens to love escargot, and orders it at every opportunity on cruises. I still refuse to cook it at home. It reminds me too much of the giant banana slugs in my garden, but to each his own. He says the garlic butter is the best part. Can we just eat garlic butter and skip the dead snails? I tell him, "Consider them a treat you can only eat on cruise ships." Hey, wait a minute...is that why he keeps booking cruises??

If you find you dislike something you ordered, politely let your waiter know. You do not need to inquire as to whether your steak previously won many horseraces, or cast aspersions on the chef's parentage; just nicely request something else, please. The staff actually wants you to be happy ---their reviews depend on it---so if you ordered squab and think it tastes like a dead pigeon, feel free to ask for the pork instead.

Enlist the Waiter

Ask for the water's recommendation for dinner items; they saw the food today, and you didn't. If they say the lamb is delicious, and the beef not so good, get the lamb.

Waiters can be a resource for other things, too, such as what not to miss in port tomorrow, or where to buy decent souvenirs. They seem to have time off in ports more than other staff and crew; a couple of hours in port midday makes them near-experts.

If you are respectful and friendly to waiters, they will often tell you all sorts of things that will make your vacation better! If you are snobbish and demanding, they keep their knowledge to themselves...and you miss out.

If dinner runs late, and you have a show to catch, you can **ask for your dessert To Go**. Your waiter will bring in on a covered plate, and off you go. The first time we took our dessert into the theater, we were braced for a comment or two, but the only remark we heard was "why didn't I think of that?" Taking a dessert or drink into the theatre is fine--- taking a tray full of heaped plates from the buffet is tacky.

The wait staff are there to meet your needs. **Let waiter know your evening plans** so they can time your meal, as in, "we want to make the 8 pm show" or "tonight we'd prefer to have a leisurely meal." Waiters want you to be happy, but very few are certified mind readers. Be reasonable; you can't expect a sit-down dinner to be as speedy as fast food.

Buffets

I consider buffets rather a last resort, a place to grab a quick breakfast on our way exploring, or a snack if dinner is too far off. Some people actually prefer the buffet for dinner. They find it faster and there's no call to dress up. In fact, the buffet is often busiest on Formal Night. Personally, I like being waited on; I get my own food at home! On sea days, a leisurely breakfast in main dining room is a wonderful start to the day.

In an evening, perhaps after the show, or on your way to admire the stars, the buffet is a great place to grab a cookie or warm cobbler, or maybe a small sandwich to fill up that last corner of your stomach.

Room Service

Ah, room service! A bit of luxury for no added cost. Breakfast in bed, cheese and crackers before dinner, cookies and milk at bedtime...we just don't get that kind of pampering at home! Room Service costs no extra. There's a menu in the binder in your cabin, or on TV. We typically tip a couple of dollars for this service.

If I remember in the flurry of packing, I make up room service tips ahead of time. I wrap **a couple of dollars around a candy bar** with a rubber band, one of those full-size chocolate bars. They are flat, pack easily, and it's no trouble to tuck them into a convenient drawer to be grabbed at the knock of a door. I enjoy seeing the server's face light up when given the tip, plus a treat---guaranteed instant smile! A candy bar can easily be eaten or given away, takes minimal space, and who doesn't like an unexpected candy? I think service is faster the next time, but I could be imagining it.

If you order room service the night before, with that little door-knob hanger card in your cabin, they usually warn you 10 minutes ahead by phone. It's a nice **wake-up call.**

Have breakfast in bed, or while you're running around getting ready. The night before an early-morning port arrival, order room service, or just order juice and rolls. You won't get stuck in a long buffet line and risk missing your departure or excursion. It's a pleasant start to a day.

Our daughter went on a cruise for her honeymoon, and reported how much they enjoyed breakfast in bed with whales visible right outside the porthole. Ahh....

 Can you believe some people? Seems a significant population of passengers drink too much, stagger to their cabin late at night, call room service for some munchies, then fall dead asleep. That leaves the room service deliverer pounding on the cabin door, to no response. To counter that, several cruise lines have instituted a **late-night room service delivery fee**. Be aware of it, but I'm sure you're not that kind of person.

Complaints, Compliments, and Comments

Complaining as Needed

Things don't always go smoothly on cruise ships, or anywhere else for that matter! **Sometimes you'll encounter a genuine problem.** It's always best to tackle the issue right then and there, not wait until you get home. By then the ship has sailed, literally, and it's too late to do anything about it.

Lighten up, but **if you have a valid grievance, complain away!** On a transatlantic cruise, the cruise line had been doing maintenance in the library, and neglected to put the screws back on the heavy glass door that fronted the book shelves. We knew that when the door fell off and broke my mother's toe. Upon politely complaining, the cruise line covered her medical bills and gave her a voucher for a free cruise, since she missed out on so much on this one.

The ships are in constant competition with one another, both in the same fleet and across company lines. They really go to great lengths to please passengers and get good reviews, because it directly affects the bottom line.

Keep your complaint **polite, use names, be specific and direct**.

Stick to a single topic, not a laundry list of gripes. Those are easier to ignore, since you appear to be a Chronic Complainer.

Be sure your complaints are realistic; the ship moved and made you spill your drink, the weather was not ideal, or the waiter was taller than you prefer, will gain you only an eye roll.

Addressing your complaint to the correct person will net you far better results. Telling your cabin steward your waiter was rude will only get you sympathy, not a different waiter.

If you do have a problem, go directly to the source. If it's a cabin issue, the Hotel Director is only a phone call away. If it's a food-and-beverage problem, start with the bar staff or waiter, then move on if needed to the venue manager. Complain rarely, honestly, and calmly, and only as required.

For example, I ordered a virgin peach daiquiri in a lounge, as I watched Husband (alias The Cruise Addict) participate in a dance class. I try not to make a fool of myself in public; I'm a much better audience than dancer. The drink never came. The hour long class ended; still no drink. I could do without the frozen drink, but the server had taken my key card, and vanished. I spoke to the bar manager. He promptly tracked down the key card, apologized profusely, and comped my drink. Easy solution.

Above all, **if you have a problem, address it on the spot.** It's not fair to wait until you get home from the cruise, then write a scathing review online, when you never said a word onboard. Give them a chance to make things right!

Compliments

 Cruise lines, as well as specific ships, respond **well to compliments.** We had a not-great experience on a cruise, and opted to try other lines in the future. However, we had previously purchased a discount on an upcoming cruise with that same line. Not wanting to waste it, we booked a cruise six months later on the same ship, with low expectations. Whew— there was such a difference! The things that had irked us previously were nowhere to be seen. The morale in the staff and crew was noticeable higher, the ships was cleaner, entertainment had improved, service was better---it was dramatic!   At home, I wrote a brief, specific email complimenting the cruise line. The personal reply included an onboard credit of $25 on our next cruise ---not bad for a four-minute email! It also promised Welcome Aboard Amenities, whatever that means...I'll find out in a month, on our next cruise.

Comment Cards

The best way to reward a hard-working, friendly staff or crew member is with a **glowing review on a comment card**. Those are carefully read, and used to award prizes, like extra time off, and bonuses. They count a great deal towards promotions. A crew member even confided the best ones are posted in the crew-only areas! Just do it; it matters greatly to them, and takes you under three minutes to write.

I'm not good with names; I'm just not. I often write my comment cards on the last day of a cruise. By then it's not likely I will recall the nice bartender who made my virgin peach daiquiri just right on the first day, or the smiling clerk in the shop who helped me choose a more flattering color for my third pashmina. **Take time to jot down the names of outstanding crew and staff**, so you don't have to rack your vacation-melted brain over the comment card.

Several cruise lines are doing away with paper comment cards, instead using an **online version** a week or so after your cruise. They may only survey a select sampling of passengers, not everyone. If you have a complaint or comment, by all means, write or e-mail the cruise line directly. Contact information is on their websites, so you can direct it to the right people.

Crew, Staff, and People in Uniforms

Respect the Crew!

Chat with the crew, or at least smile at them! Not just your room steward and the waiters, but greet any crew you see working on the ship; engineers, security staff, entertainment officers, cooks/chefs, all of them. Don't tie up time or keep them from work, though.

If you treat staff and crew with the respect they deserve, you'll have a better cruise. You know they tell horror stories about "those awful passengers." Don't be them.

We make a point of smiling and greeting every one of them. In return, they feel free to reach out to us. Several stewards and waiters have thanked us and commented at the end of a cruise "you are fun! I liked being able to joke with you." If you walk by, head held at a disdainful angle, why would they approach you?

Once they learn we're just people, they tend to **go out of their way to make our cruise better.** In Maui, our steward cautiously ventured "May I suggest..? " "Of course!" She instantly lightened up and told us to walk 300 feet past the ship, around the fence, and look in the water. OH! It was where the electrical plant discharged its warm water, and there were dozens of massive sea turtles, warming up and mating. Had we not even made eye contact, we would have missed out.

If you respect the crew and staff and treat them as people instead of servants, they'll be nicer to you, and that can help **when you really need something**, like advice on the port, a lime, tweezers, superglue, or help clasping your necklace.

Remember to take the time to say "good morning/afternoon/evening" "thank you" and **use your manners like your mama taught you**. If you are a little bit better behaved than the average cruiser, you will likely be treated a little bit better.

Most of the staff are very happy to talk with passengers, and you'll hear some great stories about life on board, life at home, interesting facts about the ship, hints and tips about upcoming ports, the best places to grab a bite onshore or buy wonderful items you just don't see at home.   The ship is their home!

But There Are Boundaries...

Remember that **the crew is there to do a job, not to become your new Best Friend**. They live in very small quarters, and really don't have space for the trinkets passengers bring them from home as gifts. Really, would *you* appreciate a t shirt from somebody else's hometown? Or a perfume that's not of your liking?

I know of a passenger who buys heaps of mittens from a discount store to give the crew, "because they're going to Alaska and might be cold. They always tell me thank you." Not good, on several fronts: the crew *knows* their next stop, and prepares accordingly, the cruise line provides cold weather uniforms and clothing as needed, discount store mittens are not all that warm, and *of course* they say thank you---they're *trained* to be polite!!

Wouldn't <u>you</u> prefer to choose your own cap, or gloves, or mug, or t-shirt, or toiletries, as you desire? **Don't burden the crew** with things they don't need, can't store and would sooner choose themselves.

Tips are greatly appreciated; you can't go wrong with a couple of dead presidents, if you think your crew has gone above and beyond. They work really hard, for long hours for surprisingly low pay, with very little time off, and genuinely appreciate even small tips. Or larger ones, for that matter. Rather than spending $20 on things they just don't need, put the $20 in an envelope. It's much more welcome, and one size fits all.

We went snorkeling off Maui, and one of us had a tough time fitting swim fins over her water shoes. Okay, it was me, and by the time I wrestled them on, the surf had filled my swimsuit with a remarkable amount of sand. We're talking several *cups* of sand. Naturally, I needed a shower after the day's adventure, and it all fell out when I stepped into the shower. Wet sand is hard to scoop up discreetly with only a washcloth. Instead, I apologized to our steward, who smiled and said, "No problem, I've seen worse!" I doubted that. **Going above and beyond, dealing with extra messes, etc, deserves an extra tip.**

Roll Calls and Meet-and-Greets

Get involved onboard, months or weeks before the ship even sails. Join an online roll call for your particular cruise. Go to CruiseCritic.com, then communities, then forums; follow links to your specific cruise line, ship, then date. Read to catch up, then jump in with your introduction. It's a safe place to ask questions and "meet" other passengers before you sail. We've organized small-group private tours ahead of time, made plans to meet at sail away, as well as gathering tons of pertinent information on the ports and ship. Need an idea for what to do in port, or a ping-pong partner? Roll calls often step up.

 A Roll Call will very often organize an onboard gathering, usually on the first sea day, called a **Meet and Greet** or **Meet and Mingle** (depending on cruise line). It's nice to put faces to names, after communicating online. Some cruise lines go all out, providing snacks, drinks, prize drawings, and a chance to meet senior staff and officers. The gatherings are usually under an hour. It's a good opportunity to meet some other passengers in a small group setting, as well as making eye contact with the senior staff.

That's handy if you have An Issue later on. Seems **if they know you are internet-savvy, they go out of their way to make you happy**, in fear of a negative online review. On Day One of a cruise, as were we unpacking, I noticed the corner table in the cabin had a thick layer of oily dust on it. Made me edgy; if the steward missed that table, what else had not been cleaned? Certainly I could have wiped it off myself, but I chose instead of politely mention it to the Hotel Director after the Meet and Greet. I tell you, all week, staff and crew I didn't even know made a point of greeting me and asking if all was to my satisfaction!

You never know what might happen at a Meet and Greet.
Make the effort to be there! On a coastal cruise, we noticed the whole staff and crew seemed a little uneasy. One finally admitted the new Captain had been onboard as long as we had! Not knowing his style yet, they were wary. "The only thing we know about him is that he hung a huge Swedish flag in his office. You know how strict Swedes are!" At the Meet and Greet, the Captain strode in briskly, without even a smile. He glared at his staff, who promptly stood up straighter. The Captain nodded at us passengers, barked "A Bridge tour for all of you! Complain to my staff if you must," and stalked out, as abruptly as he arrived. The Security officer gasped, "THAT never happens!" It was a great tour; we had over an hour to ask questions and be taught by the Second in Command the following afternoon. Midway through the week, we overheard the Captain joking with the Cruise Director. All was well.

Cruise Across Generations

Plan for the Whole Clan

A cruise is a great vacation for a **multi-generational** get together! There's plenty for everyone to do, no one has to cook or entertain the relatives, and a ship is big enough if *too much* togetherness becomes a problem.   Compare costs; by the time you book a beach house for the whole family tree, and buy all that food, and reserve theatre tickets for everybody, it'll cost more than just taking them all on a cruise.

I have a friend who dislikes Christmas shopping. Last year, she gave her relatives tickets for a five-day Mexican Rivera cruise, instead of traditional gifts. All thirty-seven of them! They made memories, and not one of those gifts was returned.

A ship allows so much flexibility. The old folks can nap in the afternoon, the kids can enjoy the children's programs, the young ones can dance the night away, and everybody meet back for dinner. Without the stress of having to entertain at your home, you can **see your extended family in a whole new light** on a ship. We had a nephew go from being a staid missionary to winning the onboard cross-dressing beauty contest on a cruise just a week later. I felt awkward, telling him his skirt was too short, and to please hold his beaded purse front and center...but *somebody* had to say it!

If you're in charge of booking a large group cruise, say for Great Grandma and her descendants, **rely on a good travel agent,** preferably a brick-and-mortar one who specializes in cruises. They'll be able to suggest options you may not know about. They know which cruise lines cater to large family groups best. They do the research, you decide, they do the legwork, paperwork, and logistics, you get the perks and credit, they get any blame required, as well as handling any Issues that may arise. Everyone will think you're wonderful! ...except Aunt Julie. She never liked you anyway.

Nearly every cruise line will toss in one free cabin if you travel in a group of 15 or more or book more than seven cabins on the same sailing. **It's a nice perk for your effort in** getting everyone to agree on a date. No, you don't have to tell them...they'll never know, right?

People to Avoid Onboard

In our family, we tell the kids that **there are people onboard with whom we will not associate**, in particular the security staff and medical personnel. Sometimes they listen. Other times, we're grateful for good insurance.

Security

A cruise ship is like a small city, or maybe an island, and **Security is the ship's police force.** They will come up out of the woodwork if a problem arises, such as a skirmish or fight breaking out.

Remember **there are security cameras all around the ship!** Looking to see if the coast is clear before you do something stupid won't save you.

Security officers have the power to confine you to your cabin, or even put you and your party off the ship in the next port. Stories abound of passengers being left on shore for such infractions as throwing lounge chairs into the sea, punching out the Cruise Director, and letting their kids run absolutely amok. It's just much easier and less costly to just behave yourselves.

Security cameras are everywhere on ships, except in your cabin and in public restrooms. Once we attended the Newlywed Game onboard. One of the questions was "where is the strangest place you've ever made whoopee?" One couple sheepishly confessed, "Yesterday, on the aft elevator, between decks six and seven." The cruise director promptly exclaimed, "Yeah, we <u>know!</u>" Confine your amorous activities to your cabin. Please!

Don't be flashy with your valuables such as jewelry, cash, or expensive electronics; this can make you a target, same as anywhere on land.

Medical Staff

Another set of people we try hard to avoid associating with is **the medical team**. Every ship has a medical staff, and office hours, with a doctor and nurses on call. The office is supplied with various medicine and equipment to handle minor and mid-sized medical adventures, such as cuts, bruises, infections, twisted knees, broken bones, sprains, and some illnesses. A ship cannot manage major things such as stroke, heart attacks, and major injuries. Several of our cruises involved a passenger or two getting airlifted off the ship for a larger medical issue. Be flexible, be grateful it's not you, and don't holler if an emergency requires a change in plans, or even a missed port.

Watch--- a healthy passenger contingent will board with you, and by the end of any cruise, a sizable portion will be in slings, braces, or on crutches. Dance, play, be involved, but **keep your wits about you.** And be warned that the first question you'll be asked upon arrival at the Medical Center is "How much have you had to drink?"

Unfortunately, expect occasional rude behavior from your fellow passengers, no matter what cruise lines you are on. No one knows why they paid to be grouchy on a vacation; they could have been grouchy at home for free. **Keep your sense of humor, and never retaliate**; you are better than that. Don't fall into the it-doesn't-matter-what-I-do-I'll-never-see-these-people-again trap. You have to live with yourself, and you are A Nice Person, right?

Take an Extra Day or two

Arrive in your port city a day ahead of time; it's the cheapest insurance you can buy, and it will save massive stress. It gives you time to rest up, adjust to a new time zone, and get a feel for the embarkation city. We, with all of our kids, were to fly from Seattle to meet my parents in Tampa, then drive to Miami, where my brother's family would join us for a Caribbean cruise. This was back before e-tickets, and everybody's tickets had been mailed to me. A reasonable plan, until the snow began to pile up. We ended up leaving about 12 hours early for the airport, frantic that the flight would be delayed. We made it, but if worrying burns calories, I would have been a size 2 that day!

Consider staying an extra day after disembarking, or at least book a flight later in the day. Rushing to catch a flight is a lousy way to wrap up a relaxing cruise, not to mention ships are often delayed by port closures, weather, slow customs agents, etc. Missing a flight is a needless stressor, and an extra vacation day is *never* a bad thing.

Stretch a Little

At home, you tend to go about doing what you always do, barely making eye contact with other humans. You're on vacation, away from home. Get into the spirit of things! **Make new friends onboard**! After a few days, you'll note that people begin to look familiar. Greet them, be warm and outgoing, more so than at home. A greeting of "is this your first cruise?" is a universal conversation-starter.

Frequent cruisers often have tricks you'd like to know, and first-timers' enthusiasm is contagious. Often, you'll learn something new, and you might even get a tip for your next once-in-a-lifetime cruise. Realizing that people from all over are generally decent is a good lesson to remember. **Talk to people!**

They may learn something from you, too. We noticed a family was following us in a port one day, about twelve feet behind us. They never said a word, just stopped when we stopped and walked when we walked, averting their eyes when we glanced back. Finally, the man confessed, "you look like you know where to go and what to do, and we don't. Hi, I'm Tom, and this is my family." We enjoyed a couple of pleasant hours together. It pays to plan ahead.

Go and do the things that might be a little out of your "interest zone." Talk to people you meet, try foods that you might not necessarily order at home, experience new things. The whole point of a cruise vacation is to step off the world, and out of your routine. If you do the same things, eat the same things, act the same way as you do at home, well, why did you come on a cruise?

Weather or Not

Inclement weather brings out the complainers onboard; you have them at home, too. I choose to **ignore the weather**. I'm from western Washington, where perfect weather is the stuff of dreams. Put on a jacket or rain poncho, or gloves as needed, but don't sulk. Go, do, don't waste the day! You may never get back there again.

Buy cheap **rain ponchos** at the dollar store before you leave home. Buy a couple; they rip, and really can't be used more than one day. It's a good idea to always bring them along when you're in port, even if it is sunny when you leave the ship. The weather can change very quickly, especially in the Caribbean. I was drenched, making a 400 foot dash to shelter when a single cloud let loose on an otherwise sunny day. I was every bit as wet as the fish in the sea. Dried in ten minutes flat, though.

Yes, **you'll look like a walking trash bag in your poncho**, but it beats being soaked and/ or freezing. And it's less bulky to carry than an umbrella. I'm from western Washington, and we don't DO umbrellas. Lots of gortex; no umbrellas. It rains nine months of the year and drips off the cedar trees the other three months, but it's a pride issue with us. Only tourists carry umbrellas here.

Some of our best memories are of a **Really Bad Day in Alaska**. A serious storm was brewing, so bad that the outer decks were closed later that day as winds reached 80 knots (hurricane force, anywhere else!). We were with our young adult kids, a daughter in law, and one grandchild. Suddenly, somebody had the bright idea to go swimming! "After all," my son argued," the pool is heated, and we'll have it all to ourselves. Just look at those waves!" Reluctantly, I went along with the plan. Family memories, remember?

Grandchild happily trotted off to the Children's Program; her mother thought she didn't have enough body mass to stay warm in such weather. The rest of us donned bathing suits and braved the gale-force winds and sideways rain. Daughter in law and I took refuge in the hot tub...which was not all that hot, in that wind. The pool had whitecaps, and my family yelled in delight, "it's a wave pool!" It was; waves washed over the sides, flooding the teak deck. A few minutes into this, they decided to jump into the pool, all at once. I watched them line up, Husband (alias The Cruise Addict), son, daughter, son, all holding hands. Count of three, and they jumped.

Well, *that* was not expected! You know how pools work. You jump in; the water splashes up, then straight down, every time, right? Not this time. They jumped; the combined splash went straight up---then *sideways,* about three feet above the deck, carried by the wind. It took out the unfortunate bartender standing thirty feet away. He had a jacket on, but it did not save him from a thorough drenching.

Just then, the ship's photographer appeared (two minutes late, in my opinion!). He said something about "fools in the pool"---it was hard to hear over the roaring wind, but hey, those were MY fools in the pool, I'll have you know! He took a few shots, then retreated out of the storm. We found the photos posted in the photo shop later on. My face looked like I had some serious G-forces, not attractive! But how often can you say you swam in Alaska in hurricane force winds on a cruise ship with your family? Some memories are worth the pain. Pain? That was the part about making my way out of the hot tub across the blustery deck!

Staying Shipshape

Along with the restaurants and buffets and grills and 24 hour food service, **every cruise ship has a fitness center, and most have a jogging track** as well. Many have enviable fitness equipment, with much better scenery that your local gym at home. Classes are also offered, such as yoga, spinning, and aerobics. Some classes have fees and scheduled times, as shown in your daily "mail."

 Street shoes are not allowed in the gym area, or in workout classes, so pack some work out type shoes if you're interested. You should not be on a treadmill in those cute heels, anyway.

As the morning progresses on sea days, the running track becomes congested and becomes the walking track. I've even seen people even drag loungers onto the track! **If you want to do serious running, or even jogging, get there early.**

Look for a sign posted on the wall near the jogging track to learn how long it is. Some are decent; I've seen others that say "14 laps= one mile." I think I'd be dizzy long before I reached my goal!

If you plan to use the ship's fitness center or jogging track, you'll want to **bring exercise clothing**. Tee shirts and shorts will be fine. Many people recommend a poly wicking fabric that dries quickly.

You can rinse it out and not have heaps of **smelly sweaty clothes ripening** under the bed. Hands wash your workout clothing immediately after use, or take it in the shower with you. Hang on the clothesline in the bathroom. Ventilation is pretty good—they'll be dry before morning.

If you're able and not going far, **consider skipping the elevators in favor of taking the stairs**. You can burn calories, often save time, and free up the elevators for those who really need them.

Our second cruise was on the old *Norway*, which was configured for social classes. That meant everywhere we wanted to be was at the far end of the ship, up five decks, and the elevator didn't go there. I can tell you, by the third day, my legs were screaming from the imposed effort to get them in shape!

Living in a Stateroom

A cruise cabin is probably smaller than any hotel room you've ever stayed in, but a lot more efficient. It's a common joke that if you drop your washcloth in the bathroom, it's instant wall-to-wall carpeting. When we were designing our house some years ago, we spent quite a bit of time touring mobile home dealers. Mobile homes are designed to maximize space, to make a small room seem bigger. We picked up many tactics, such as the bow window in the dining room, the cathedral ceiling in the living room, the open pass-through and half wall in the kitchen, the open flow into four main rooms. Cruise ship cabins are like that...not large, but the space is well used.

Storage

 Storage in your cabin will seem at first to be at a premium; keep looking around. We constantly find new storage spots around the room; for example, drawers under the foot of the bed , over the sofa, inside the vanity chair, or on the sides of the vanity mirror. Check behind mirrors in cabins for extra storage space ---often shelves are hidden there.

Your suitcases take up the most room. I stuff our empty ones under the bed, first thing, out of the way.

Oh, that's another tip; be sure to scour the cabin as you pack up to go home. I **pull out drawers, peek under the bed**, I mean everywhere, to be sure I'm not leaving anything behind. A friend told of an odd discovery stuffed back behind a drawer, a bra the size of a hammock. One never knows.

I sleep better on ships than anywhere else; might be the motion of the seas. If you find your bed is too hard, **request an egg crate from your cabin steward.** These foam pads are in limited supply, so ask early, soon after you first flop on your bed to try it out. You can also request extra pillows. Some cruise lines even have a pillow *menu.*

Each cabin has its own temperature control, so you probably won't need to request more blankets. Be sure to **close your balcony door if the air conditioning is on**, or it won't work.

You'll work out your own system for **keeping track of your small items**. Those little paper caps on the drinking glasses in your cabin make great holders for coins, earrings, and other little belongings. Small zip lock bags are handy, or you can even bring a shallow tray from home.

At the end of the day, I choose shoes for the next day, and pile whatever I need in one of them by the door; key card, reading glasses, maybe cash or cell phone for shore, etc. Some folks always bring a hat, whether they look good in one or not. At the end of the day they can throw all of their stuff in it, ready to grab in the morning.

Remove unused clothes hangers in the cabin's closet. As the ship moves, they get very noisy at night.

Keeping Track of Time

Leaving your **cell phone** on just to tell time can run up roaming charges, even if you never dial it. If you choose to use it for a clock, remember to put it in **Airplane Mode**.

Consider bringing a battery operated **alarm clock** for cabin. Plug-in ones vary a lot in the timekeeping, due to the ship's alternating power. Your plug- in clock may run very slow or jump ahead 45 minutes. A battery operated clock will ensure you don't miss that all important towel folding demo.

Nightlights

I value my shins, so I bring a **nightlight** of some sort on cruises. We've learned that NCL has a small light in the back of the closets that leaks just enough light to act as nightlight. You could pick up a small light at the Dollar store at home, or **leave bathroom door barely ajar** with towel over the top to prevent slamming when the ship moves. It's also a good idea to **loop a glow stick** on the bathroom doorknob.

Oh, yes, the chocolate story! We were cruising with another couple. They were late to breakfast, and Natalie seemed quite flustered when they finally arrived. Damp, too. We pried the story out of her; it's what friends do. Seems her husband had gone to bed early the previous night, while Natalie went to admire the stars. By the time she made her way to the cabin, Jim was snoring, with the lights off. She is much more considerate than most people –certainly more than I—so she silently slipped into bed, in the pitch dark. Natalie awoke in the morning, with an odd sensation on her head. Upon investigation, she discovered her hair was glued to the pillow!

She pried her hair free, turned on a light, and was aghast to see chocolate on her pillow, sheet, mattress, face, nightclothes, and of course in her hair. Jim woke up suddenly to see his chocolate-covered wife frantically scrubbing the bedding. Seems the steward left extra chocolate on their pillows the night before, and Jim thoughtfully scooped *his* candies onto Natalie's pillow, and in the dark, well.

The cabin steward assured them he had cleaned up much worse, and offered to put the nightly chocolate on the desk, henceforth. We suspect he had a good laugh, but he was kind enough to do it out of earshot.

This tip reminds you to bring a nightlight, or prop your bathroom door open just a little, with the light on.

Land Ho!

Port Days

Sea days are great, but there's something exciting about reaching a new port. It lays ahead of you, full of potential for adventure! If you have a scheduled tour, you'll need to join the crowd, when it seems most of the passengers want to get off the ship first thing. If you can, wait a few minutes after the doors open, to let crowds go their way. You can leave at your leisure, without getting jostled.

In ports, **you may come and go off the ship as you please**, so long as you are back on before the time posted by the gangway for sail away. Often, we've gone exploring in the morning, came back to the ship for lunch and a 15 minute rest, then back out in the afternoon.

I think **it's best to start your day early**, in case you find Something Amazing onshore. How sad would it be to run out of time, because you lazed by the pool all morning and got onshore very late? You can always get back on if you run out of things to do.

Do people really run out of things to do??

Be sure you and your family members **know the name of your ship**. Sounds obvious? I've seen this happen quite a few times; passengers wait in line to board the ship in a port, and are politely told their ship is the one across the pier, not this one. They all wear the same sheepish expression as they hustle past everyone!

Hint: the **ship's name is printed** right on your key card.

Need advice on where to get the best local cuisine on shore? Ask a hotel doorman, or a sales clerk in a small store. Cabbies and concierges are often on commission; they get a few bucks for every tourist who mentions them. You want good food, not expensive food.

As you plan your activities, **pay attention to which days your ship will be in port.** One day is pretty much like another on a cruise ship, but onshore, it matters. You should factor in a bit more travel time if you overlap a rush hour on weekdays. On Sundays, be aware than many shops and attractions such as museums will be closed. Sunday might be a better day to hike, enjoy a beach, or appreciate what Nature put there for you to value. On the other hand, don't assume anything; we enjoyed a tour through a state capitol on a very rainy Labor Day. Our dinner partners assumed it would be closed, and missed out. Do your homework before you leave home.

Ship life is cashless, but ports are not. Remember to take your cash and or credit card with you when you leave the ship, because you can't buy that lovely necklace or mango gelato with your key card! It's been tried. No, not by me.

Open your eyes to options you had not considered as you arrive in a new port. Frequently, you'll find helpful brochures and detailed maps, or even local people ready to make your visit to their home town memorable. Being flexible often leads to serendipity.

Don't feel like going into port today? I can't imagine you'd have really seen it all last time, but if you choose to stay onboard while the ship is parked, you'll find a different experience. Since most passengers go exploring, the ship will seem quieter. There will be fewer activities scheduled on port days. Often, special prices will be offered in the ship's spa.

Beach Tips

A waterproof case that will go around your neck or inside your swimsuit can hold your ID, cruise card, credit card, cash, etc, while swimming, eliminates the need for a Designated Beach Sitter to keep watch over the belongings on the beach.   Place your stuff into a zip lock bag first, as added insurance.

Bring beach shoes to protect against rocky shores & jellyfish, if your cruise goes where beaches are. A slit toe can spoil a trip, fast.

Don't bother packing **beach towels**. The ship provides them for use onboard, as well as onshore. Be aware, that some mainstream cruise lines have begun exacting a fee for lost or misplaced towels, up to $25!

Rather than keep track of a towel, or dispute the charges on the last day, I **consider beach towels our first souvenir.** The bright ones with a map of the island are my favorites. They're thin, dry fast, and certainly stand out!

Dry meat tenderizer is a quick remedy against the pain of a hungry jellyfish. Fits nicely in your beach bag, too.

Those fancy "waterproof" containers for valuables while swimming can leak. Take a few **sandwich size zip lock baggies** and put your stuff in (S/S card, cash, etc), squish all the air out, and then put it in your waterproof container...works great!

If you're planning on a lot of swimming or beach days**, take two bathing suits per person**. That way, while you're waiting for a wet one to dry, you've got a dry one to wear. Clammy swimsuits feel icky. And please bring a cover-up, or at least a long t shirt...no one wants to be that close in a crowded elevator!

If you're buying a new swimsuit for the cruise, **read the care label.** I'm puzzled by the Dry Clean Only labels on some swimwear!

Snorkeling

If you plan to go snorkeling on your cruise, buy **disposable underwater cameras** at your local discount store before you leave. We paid $6 for ours at home, and they were selling for $28 on the ship, $23 on shore.

Another snorkeling tip: even when you are super excited about seeing so many brilliantly colored fish and turtles and sea life---way more than your local aquarium---**don't open your mouth to holler** "Wouldja look at that!?" underwater. I nearly drowned in Hawaii, pointing out a sea turtle the size of my dining room table, *right there.* That rule about they have gills, we have lungs...still applies.

Bring your own snorkeling gear, if you plan to snorkel in more than one port. Swim fins can be bulky, but at least bring your own mask and snorkel. You won't have to worry about returning the rented ones on time, or hoping the dive shops still have some available when you arrive. Don't think about how many mouths have been on those rental ones.

Bags Ashore

Take a tote bag or small backpack onshore with you, with the things you'll need for the day in port. I hate carrying needless things, so I keep mine very basic. It might contain sunscreen, sunglasses, a wrap, wipes, a few assorted zip lock bags, and a thin rain poncho. Weather is often unpredictable.

You might want to **avoid carrying or wearing anything with the ship's name or logo on it**. It marks you as an obvious tourist, and that can make you easy prey for crime. The Bad Guys can see at a glance you're not local, and they'll instantly know you'll be gone in a few hours. What are the chances you'd waste that precious short time tracking down police or a petty thief?

It might also save you some money. I carried my bag with the ship's logo in our first port on our first cruise. A shopkeeper told me with a grin, "I'd offer you the I'm-not-from-around- here discount, but you're carrying your sell-me-something bag. If you can afford a fancy cruise, you got no bargaining power with me." Bargaining is a skill worth keeping!

 Pack a few plastic bags to quickly **stash your electronics**, camera, etc. My brother's camera was found floating in the bottom of the tote bag when the water bottle's cap wiggled loose in St Thomas. Water poured out of it like a cartoon drawing! Since then, we use **zip lock plastic bags to keep the camera, e-reader, and so forth, separate from the water bottles and damp swimsuits.**

If you ignore the previous tip, and find your camera or cell phone swimming in a pond in the bottom of your tote bag, you may be able to save it. What have you got to lose? **Acquire a bowl of plain dry rice** from the ship's galley ---plead with the head waiter---and bury your dead electronic item in it for a few days. Your steward may wonder why you have a bowl of dry rice in your cabin when there is a perfectly good dining room on board, but if it saves you replacement costs...he'll get over it.

Rental Cars in Ports

Renting a car in a port is often the cheapest, easiest way to cover the turf you want to see, especially in Hawaii and other stateside ports. Reconsider in places that could be scary, like Mexico...have you *seen* those roads??

Think twice, too, in places where they drive on the "wrong" side of the road. Those intersections can be dicey.

If you rent a car, **join the rental company's loyalty program** before you book, back when you are in Price Comparing mode. It'll net you great deals, save time in long lines when you pick up the car, and costs nothing! A couple of times, we have found such good prices that when we went to pick up the car, even the agent was surprised. Book a rental car ahead of time. It'll cost less, and sometimes agencies run out of cars when ships are in port.

With a rental car and a planned route, it's often best to **jump ahead and start from the end of the route, and work your way back.** The buses and other tours will start at the nearest point and make their way to the farthest point, then drive straight back. I don't know why; but they all do. If you drive to the far end first, hopscotching the route backwards, you'll miss all of the crowds. It also gives you the peace of mind of being nearer the ship at the end of the day, instead of way out in who-knows-where with a short time to reach the port.

We did this in the Yukon, and it's a magical memory. We downloaded a mile-by-mile guide, drove out of Skagway about 70 miles into the Yukon, using utmost willpower to refrain from stopping at obviously interesting places. When we reached our planned turn-back point, we explored, then made our way back leisurely, stopping as desired. The silence was deafening, scenery gorgeous, wildlife awesome! We were utterly alone for hours---it was delightful! Finally, at the Yukon sign, we ran into five buses full of slow-moving tourists. We got our photo, and went in opposite directions. I guarantee we had a better day than they did.

Is Sleep Overrated?

You may want to put some sleep on your plan-for-the-cruise, at least a few hours here and there, if you're doing your own driving. There was that time in Hawaii, when a few hours of sleep might have saved a lot of paperwork. We set our alarm clock for 2am, and drove our rental car up to Haleakala, hoping to be in place in time to see a great sunrise. The sunrises only happen about once out of nine times. The rest of the time, the sky just gradually lightens and day begins. We had high hopes. And three hours of sleep under our belts.

The sunrise was magnificent! I've never seen such oranges and golds and pinks and reds. Mother Nature put on a show for us, water colors against the sky. We applauded as the rim of the sun peeped over the crater, along with dozens of other crazy tourists. Just awesome!

The road up was hairpin turns, as the road rose from sea level to 10,000 feet altitude. It was the same on the way down, and that was reasonable. The trouble was when we reached the straight, level section of road on the bottom. Husband (alias The Cruise Addict) was driving, and telling a story. He was literally speaking, when he fell asleep and rammed the car in front of us. My screaming didn't wake him in time. He'd had three hours of sleep, out of the last ...um, maybe 30 hours. We like to Go and Do, but we're not robots. A nap would have been a good idea.

Lighten up! In the aforementioned story, we could have let the wrecked car ruin the day, or the rest of the cruise. Instead, we dealt with the police, tow truck, car rental agency, insurance company, then went snorkeling. It made a good story.

Oh, another tip---**listen to the experts**, in this case, the park ranger. He warned us that the 10,000 foot altitude was not to be messed with. "Walk, don't run, take it slow, breathe, and if you feel even a little lightheaded, LIE DOWN. Right there; don't head for your car. Don't sit down. You can still crack your head while sitting. If you faint, and hit your head, you will bleed, I will call the ambulance, it will split the glorious silence with that caterwauling siren, and you will be hauled off to the hospital where they will treat you with rusty needles, and spoil your vacation. Take it easy." Guides and local people know way more than you do. Count them as resources, wherever you go!

Planning Ahead of Time

Our friends call me 'Information Booth.' I would feel terrible to return home and learn that most wonderful thing was *right there* and I missed it!

Consequently, I **research, read up on the area, study maps, and plan in advance.** If I'm going to go that far, and spend that much, I want to enjoy it. A good part of that enjoyment is triggered by prior planning. I want to be the most well-read person on the ship.

If you booked your cruise out far enough ---a few of ours have been very short-notice—this tip will help you plan your day in that port. **Get online, and do a search** for the city's name, and tourism, like "Boston tourism." Offers to send you brochures will pop up, and you'll find them helpful as you plan. It's fun to see pretty pictures and dream a little, too. Just think, soon, you'll be right there!

Planning is part of the fun---it just builds the anticipation of another cruise!

You'll talk about your cruise vacation for the rest of your life, so make it good! In my opinion, **great vacations don't just "happen" - you have to PLAN for them**. This doesn't mean you have to plan every second of your day; certainly spontaneity can be awesome. Although it feels like a lot of planning, especially before your first cruise, you're trading planning in the comfort of your home with worry and nuisance on your vacation. Once you're on board all of the worry goes away. I know folks who do **spreadsheets** on the Plan For The Day and post them on the cabin's walls; that's just overboard. Or it ought to be. There's a nice wide middle ground between compulsive over-planning and flying by the seat of your pants.

We have a **file folder** labeled TRIPS. Currently, it has papers about four upcoming cruises, a beach-house family gathering, and that weekend away Husband (alias The Cruise Addict) promised for my birthday. Papers for each trip are neatly paper -clipped together. As we plan, we add brochures about places we want to see when we're there, reservations for tours we booked ahead of time, local maps, cruise documents, car rental reservations, and any e-tickets for planes, trains, hot air balloons, and so forth. When we pack for a trip, the file folder slips into a carry-on bag.

Take a labeled manila envelope for each port or day. In each, place any shore excursion tickets, car rental papers, maps, and a note of what you especially want to see that day. At the end of the day, add in any brochures, maps, and the ship's daily schedule, along with receipts for anything you bought onboard. Instant record of the trip!

Our last cruise to Hawaii was so packed, it required a folder for each day! We exchanged knowing glances over breakfast each morning when the cruise line's Ambassador told of options for exploring the island, as she said "Of course, there is no way you can visit all these places" knowing full well we could and we would. We rented a car in every port, and had the days planned out, along with some time for goofing off. Not all that much...I realized I may have gone overboard, so to speak, when we pulled into the parking lot of a Top Ten In The World beach and I heard myself say, "we have two hours and forty minutes to relax here, so get busy!"

And there was that day in an overnight port when the only time we had for snorkeling was at 6 am. Actually, now that I think about it, I recommend that. We had the peaceful cove all to ourselves, just us and a swarm of brilliant fish and some sea turtles. As I surfaced, two full-spectrum rainbows arched right overhead the pristine beach.   I felt pity for those other passengers, asleep on the ship, missing all that!

Overdoing?

Best in-port advice: **Do as much as you can.** How often are you going back there?

This rarely backfires, but I admit it can. On a cruise that stopped in Astoria, we rented a car ahead of time. In seven hours, we visited three WWII forts, with visitor's centers, toured the Maritime Museum (rated top ten in the US), drove to the very point where the Columbia River meets the Pacific Ocean and climbed the lookout tower there (calm on the river side, wild on the ocean side---quite a contrast!), climbed the Astoria Column, stopped for clam chowder (and *chili*—The Cruise Addict loves chili), leisurely shopped at an open-air market, walked along the promenade and poked in some little shops, and saw the *Peter Iredale* shipwreck (right on the beach!). We're going back next month...and the Cruise Addict and I have discussed, "what shall we do in Astoria? It's a tiny place, and I think we saw it all!"

A Ship's Shore Excursion, or DIY?

You can go off **exploring on your own in ports, or take a shore excursion tour** booked through the cruise line. Obviously, on your own, you'll have much more freedom and flexibility. Overly cautious cruisers may prefer a ship's shore excursion, but be warned—it'll cost a lot more.

An advantage to a ship-sponsored tour is that it has been vetted for safety and professionalism, whatever that means. In a risky tour, that *can* make a difference. You don't want to book a fly-by-night jungle zip line, only to find it's some guy with a rope in his backyard. Just do your homework before you book any tour.

Ship sponsored shore excursions are often over-priced and over-crowded. You can get much better quality for a bargain price -- and don't believe the "you'll be left behind on an island" scare tactic. Shore excursions are a huge money-maker for the cruise line; naturally, they push passengers to book through them. You can read a wristwatch, right?

Local tour operators are very aware of your **need to get back to the ship on time**. They know you may well post a review online to God and everybody that they made you miss the ship, which would of course hurt their future income. In these days, they rely on positive online reviews. You make your way around your hometown; you can make your way around almost any cruise port!

It's a common fallacy that if you are on a ship-sponsored tour that returns to the ship late, **the ship will wait for you. Not true!** Ships do guarantee they'll see you to the next port, but that can mean they'll fly you there, not hold the ship. Ships pay for their dock space in ports; they have to go when their time is up. It's cheaper for the cruise line to fly a few passengers to the next meeting spot than pay those hefty late-in-berth fines. For many passengers, this is the main selling point of a ship's tour. I'd hate for you to plan your trip on an untruth.

If you lean towards ship sponsored shore excursions, **do your homework!** If you are absolutely heartset on a very popular tour, book it as soon as you can, from home.   Swimming with dolphins often sells out early, for example. I still suggest you **compare with private companies,** to check the cost of booking with the ship vs. booking directly with the company who offers the excursions.

Be aware that **there are some tours you really can't arrange on your own,** such as the engineer's tour of the Panama Canal. Some are at a distance you might feel uneasy traversing by mass transit. If you go to Cozumel to the ruins, I would take an excursion, because of the distance. Places in the former USSR require a ship's tour, with local guide. Places vary—yet another reason to read all about it!

Research your ports ahead of time, and reserve private excursions. We've seen motor coaches (alias buses) crammed full of cruisers, waiting for laggards to show up, stopping for a ten minute "photo op" then people herded back in longs lines to pile back on. Shudder! We find the financial savings significant over the cruise ship's mass tours, but for the us, the privacy and flexibly add so much more to the day. Being on your own, or with a small, intimate group is much more flexible and fun!

 Peggy's Cove is a popular tourist spot in Nova Scotia. It's a charming town, population thirty-five on a good day, with Canada's most photographed lighthouse. We took a private tour, two town cars with eight friends. It was a highlight of the cruise. Our group toured a maple processing plant (with tastings), spent an hour with the author of the Peggy's Cove book series *in his home*, stopped as desired for photos of gorgeous fall colors and a beaver dam, explored Peggy's Cove and the scenery, took scads of photos and admired the lighthouse, stood in awe as our driver told personal stories at the Titanic cemetery, and best of all, had two pound lobsters for lunch at picnic tables on a bay so pretty it rivaled postcards. Our drivers knew the proprietor, and those giant fresh lobsters cost less than market price. I felt sorry for the hordes of tourists in Peggy's Cove, herded *with whistles* on and off SIX big busses. Several told us the tour went straight from the ship to the Cove, and back, with no stops. They paid more than double what we paid for our tour.

Many cities have **Hop On Hop Off tours**. They tend to be double-decker busses, often open on top, with a tour guide who narrates and tells stories as the bus drives a prescribed tour. They are often storytellers and real characters, who make the sights come alive. As advertised, you may hop off at interesting places, then hop on the next bus. We like to stay on for one whole circuit first to get a feel for the city, and mentally mark the areas that warrant further exploring. These tours can be a good compromise between going off on your own, and an established tour.

A cruise is not the time to try out new shoes! Wear comfortable shoes, especially in port, when running to your cabin to change is not an option. Socks are important, too, so your sneakers don't rub you raw. Blisters are tiny, but capable of spoiling your day pretty fast.

Cabs in Ports

Some of our favorite memories include our time in the
Caribbean. In several ports, we walked off the ship, past the
inevitable gauntlet of tour-hawkers and aggressive taxi drivers.
We found a taxi with a friendly-looking driver, and told him,
"We want to see your island, the things you think we should not
miss. Will you take us?" For very low prices, we got **a private
tour with a local resident who knew where to go.** We had to
convince the driver we didn't want to see the Typical Touristy
Things, but once we accomplished that, we had a great time!
The drivers took us to out of the way museums, incredible
beaches, marinas, local markets, a 1700's slave quarters, 400
years old forts, the church where Ronald Regan worshipped on
vacation, all the while regaling us with stories, local flavor, and
history. They took time to ask what sort of things we were
interested in, and made it really intense, once they understood
we genuinely were interested in their home. Of course we had
the flexibility to stop where desired; those stuffed busses can't
do that. A private tour of the very best kind! Cost? Around $40
for five hours, for four of us!

You can always ask another couple of passengers if they'd like
to **share a taxi in port.** Cabs charge by the trip, not per person,
so it costs the same for one person as five.

If you're in a foreign port where there could be a language
barrier, be sure to **take a postcard of the ship** with you.
Showing the cab driver a picture cuts down on the always-

ineffective pantomime. Raising your voice never helps them understand your language any better, either, although I've seen many tourists try. Free postcards are often in the binder in your cabin, or pick one up at the Guest Services desk.

Ship's Shore Excursion?

Some ship-sponsored shore tours sell out fast, such as swimming with the dolphins, so if you are heart set on a particular tour, it's best to book it early. Others, you'd better wait until you can gauge the weather. For example, you can buy tickets for the tram to Mount Roberts in Juneau on the ship, or even months in advance, but it frequently clouds over. The rule there is, if you can't see the top of the mountain, there's no sense taking the tram up to the top. On a clear day, however, the tram is awesome! Plus, you can ride it as many times in a day as you choose. I still think you're way smarter to buy the tickets yourself that very day; much less costly than on the ship, and you can decide if it's a tram day, or a day for more shopping.

Always compare options, if you want to book a popular attraction. Alcatraz tickets can be bought directly from the National Park Service, but if they sell out, see if the cruise line has any left from the block they bought long ago. If the ship's tour is sold out, look locally.

Some people insist on spending the extra money for a ship's shore excursion, **but you'll very often do better on your own.** In every port, the local tour people and cabbies are very well aware of the ship's arrival, and wait like vultures. If you just walk off the ship you'll find lines of tours waiting to give you the same thing for about half the price, usually with more flexibility.

For example, you can get a bus to Mendenhall Glacier out of Juneau for $14 round trip, or pay $36 through the cruise line for a very similar bus on the exact same route. Kiosks selling those tickets, plus whale watching, dog sled camps, and glacier hikes are right past the docks.

In Halifax, we debated about taking a city tour, since it was our first visit. City tours give a good overview. Ship's tours cost $56, for two hours, and we cringed when we saw the six big busses, lined up ready to suck up hoards of people, probably 60 people each. Insult to injury, the tour didn't go to the Reversing Falls. We opted to just walk around until we found something interesting. That took the form of a guy with a sign standing by a small city bus. "City and environs tour, 3 hours, $21, guaranteed Reversing Falls." Booked it that fast! Our driver grew up in Halifax, was loaded with history and interesting facts about the area and the people who live there, and took us to more places that the ship's bus would have. He was quite a storyteller, and left us with fun memories. Due to the very small group on the bus, we even had time to wander at several places, instead of the "drive past" the ship promised. Watch for deals like that, and take a risk. **The best experts are the people who call that port home.**

Looking through the shore excursions the cruise line offers is a good place to get ideas. Check thoroughly, however, to see if it's really worth the extra cost. For example, in Ketchikan, you can book the Lumberjack show through the cruise line for $45. A woman will meet you at the gangway and walk you three blocks to the show. Or, you can walk the three blocks, and buy a ticket for $23. Same show, same seats!

Did I tell you about the market in Antigua? I asked the driver of our private tour to take us to a local market. He nodded "yes, yes, where the tourists go." No. "I want a real market, where YOU shop." It was a fine market! We are your average white folks, traveling with a friend who has stunning long blonde hair. I'm pretty sure we were the only non-local people within an eight block radius. The vendors were very nice to us! As I hastily selected spices, I realized Husband (alias The Cruise Addict) had wandered off. I quickly walked through the market, looking down each aisle. A vendor politely called, from her seat, "If you seek your Husband, he is four rows over, trying on a very nice hat with a feather." Did she see through walls, too? That market is a happy memory, and those people on the crowded tour busses never knew it was there.

Lunch in Port

Nothing wrong with you enjoying a morning in port, returning to the ship for lunch ---**you've already paid for it**---then resuming exploring onshore all afternoon. If you don't, then...

Eat local. Be where you are! Seek local dishes; you might find a new favorite. If not, hey, you have a good story to tell. Our food stories usually include Husband (alias The Cruise Addict). While I happily slurped my tofu-seafood saimin in Honolulu, he ordered enchiladas. He complained they were the worst he'd ever tasted. Let's see; Mexican food prepared by Filipinos in Polynesia; yes, that's a recipe for disaster. Not that it stopped him...Husband also had some truly terrible chili on Fisherman's Wharf in San Francisco, while the rest of us devoured our crab cakes and clam chowder with sourdough bread. In Boston, his tacos were so bad, Husband threw them away, scowling while I enjoyed my lobster roll and clam chowder. Tacos at Quincy Market ...no wonder it was not good! Husband (alias The Cruise Addict) is not very good at being where he is, culinarily speaking.

What Else Do You Need to Know?

Assorted Tips

Plan on writing postcards to the grandchildren at home? Often you will be home long before they arrive, but if you don't mind... make your job easier by addressing stickers at home. Slap one on a postcard, jot a few lines, and you won't have to carry a bulky address book.

Need to save up some spending money for your cruise? An easy way to save is to set aside any $5 bills you get back in change or come across in the months leading up to your cruise. It's fairly painless, and adds up quick!

Don't be self-conscious about your appearance in a bathing suit, or shorts, so long as you are dressed appropriately for the venue. There will be all body types aboard in all types of attire. I used to squirm in my swimsuit in public. I was cured when we cruised with a pretty friend who happens to be slim, very toned, and blonde. I noticed that all eyes were on her, not me, and it clicked. People only stare at young, gorgeous, stereotype – shaped people! As just another ordinary body on the beach, I was functionally invisible. Changed my life.

Scrapbooking supplies are not cheap! Pick up maps and brochures in each port, plus postcards of the ship (free from Guest Service desk) and use them for backgrounds when you build your cruise scrapbook at home.

In port, wrap a **rubber band around your wallet** to thwart pickpockets. Non-slid, sort of.

Dollar stores are great places to load up on necessities. Flashlight, poncho, snacks, air freshener, magnets, duct tape, OTC meds, Band-Aids, tiny first aid kits, nightlights, glow sticks, pop up hampers, on and on can all be acquired for way less than other stores, or worse yet, onboard a ship.

There's more than one sail away! The first one comes with a party, but leaving and entering each port is awesome, too. You'll get excited just seeing the fun to come. It's great to get a first glimpse of the port while still on board. Often other ships will be in port, and it's interesting to compare. You may even select the ship for your next cruise, right there.

What All Does My Cruise Fare Include?

Read, read, read! There are extra costs, beyond the number in the shiny cruise line brochure, but there is no excuse for being caught off guard!

Generally Speaking, Your Cruise Price Includes:

your cabin (also called stateroom)

room steward service

meals onboard

some beverages

snacks

use of pools and hot tubs

most entertainment

most onboard activities

games onboard

buffet

access to fitness facilities

sports court activities, including tournaments

extras like climbing wall, mini golf, and zip lines on some ships

room service on board

use of public rooms on board

some classes, demonstrations, and workshops

some parties, such as Captain's events and art auctions

dedicated kids' and teen programs

use of Library

It Generally Won't Include:

alcoholic beverages, and sodas

laundry services

shore excursions or tours

meals in specialty restaurants

gratuities, or service charges

port charges, taxes, fuel fees

trip cancellation insurance

optional on-board activities, such as cooking classes

spa and salon services

organized exercise classes (pliates, spinning, etc)

casino and bingo

airport transfers (unless pre-purchased with air/sea packages)

onboard purchases in gift and jewelry shops

professional photography (no sitting fee; you pay if you buy)

internet access

babysitting services

video arcade

phone calls off the ship (free between cabins)

satellite connection for cell phones (ship is its own cell tower)

adventures involving the medical center

Specialty Cruises

Theme Cruises Are Great (if you're included)

Watch for theme cruises. Themes might include dancers, quilters and craft groups, real estate agents, travel agents, medical conventions, bikers or bicyclists, culinary interests, religious groups, and specific music groups and genres.   Being part of the group can enhance your vacation, with additional classes, and activities booked onboard. If you are not included, you may find it intrusive. You may love being on a ship with a country music theme; I'd find it torturous. Groups can be large and obtrusive, taking over public areas on the ships, or you may not even notice them.

We were on a cruise in the Caribbean with a group of bikers. Bicyclists, not the Hell's Angels variety, although I've heard they cruise, too. In every port, they unloaded their bicycles, and took off on a 26 mile trip. The rest of the day, they acted like tourists. We watched them every day, getting more and more tanned as the days passed. We wouldn't have even known the 400 quilters were onboard, except we peeked into the meeting rooms where they sewed most of every day.   I'm pretty sure we had more fun than they did, although they did have a new quilt at the end of the week.

Sometimes, **being part of a group can benefit you**, financially. We had a cruise booked with fifteen extended family members. I heard an ad on the radio for a travel agency, offering the exact same cruise, a week later, for significantly less, plus kids cruised free. Often travel agents can buy blocks of cabins for a great price. The special price was available for listeners of that radio station only. We called a sister in law to ask if their family could change weeks. She promptly listed a chart of excuses why that would not possibly work. I said "oh, okay, it would have saved you $800 per cabin, but it's up to you." She backpedaled so fast, I could hear tires squealing! We all took the cheaper cruise, and enjoyed extra radio-listener-only benefits, besides; a galley tour, exclusive parties, and lectures by radio personalities.

As an added bonus, we met the travel agent who advertised the special on the ship, and liked him so well, that we've worked with him on dozens of cruises since that first trip. He now emails or calls us with amazing prices on cruises he thinks we might enjoy. An upcoming one is such a great deal (a balcony cabin for $230 less than an inside cabin) that he and his family are going with us. Do other people have the travel agent on speed dial, or just The Cruise Addict?

Back to Back Cruises

Back-to-back cruises can be a good deal, lower prices with a longer itinerary, but they have their pitfalls, too. What's a back-to-back? A B2B cruise might take you west to east, and then east to west the next week, and you stay in the ship in the middle. Or, you might take a B2B repositioning cruise. For example, a ship that was in the Caribbean all winter needs to get to Alaska for the summer season. You could take it from Miami to Los Angeles, then take the second leg of the back-to-back cruise from Los Angeles to Vancouver, then fly home from there. It makes for a long, lazy vacation, often at decent prices.

Back- to- back passengers have grumbled mightily about **boredom on the second leg of the cruise,** though. The menus do not vary; what was offered on Day Two is offered again on the second leg's Day Two. Entertainment is often repeated, word for word. You might not mind sitting through the production show again, but if you already heard the comedian's every bit and heard all the Cruise Director's stories, and know all the trivia questions, it gets tedious.

Oh, No, the Dream Comes to an End

Prepare To Disembark

The last night of the cruise, the cruise line gives very detailed instructions on **how to disembark,** including putting your luggage in the hall late that evening. Each cruise line varies, so be sure to read it all, or attend the disembarkation briefing. It'll also be broadcast on your in-cabin TV. Repeatedly!

Most cruise lines allow a reasonable time to **set your packed luggage in the hall for pick up**. I think some are too early. That Royal Caribbean cruise was nearly a problem. Instructions said to have luggage in the hall no later than 11pm. I intended to... but we went to dinner, to a show, played a trivia group game with new friends, the Dance It If You Know it ended at 11pm...and we still had not packed. I stayed just long enough to find out our team had won, agreed on a place to meet our friends for snacks, then literally ran through the ship to our cabin. I skidded down the corridor at 10:56 pm. The hallway was clear; the crew had obviously already gathered the luggage. A passing crew member told me sternly, "Madam, you are LATE." I retorted, "I am NOT. I have four minutes!" I think I set a world's record for speed-packing. Our suitcases were neatly outside our door at 10:59pm. I smiled as I grabbed my wrap and headed out to meet Husband (alias The Cruise Addict) and our new friends for late-night munchies on deck. There were at least a dozen other suitcases in the hall!   When we made our way to bed some time later, our luggage was gone. Whew.

As you sadly admit your fairy-tale cruise is drawing to a close, **pay attention to what gets packed where**. Last cruise, I had purchased some pure maple syrup from a maple processing plant in Nova Scotia. It somehow ended up, securely wrapped in my soft purple sweater, in the carry-on bag, not the suitcase to be checked on the flight home. The TSA confiscated my liquid amber at the airport. Mind you, they allow six inch long screwdrivers and knitting needles, but my maple syrup was a threat to national security. I bought a bottle of maple syrup at home, likely the exact same stuff. It didn't have the memory attached, though.

On the last night, when you pack up and put your things out in the hall, plan ahead! **Keep a carry-on, and put your Stuff that you'll need for the morning in it**. I pack a flat canvas bag for this purpose.

In particular, please remember to **leave out an outfit for the next day**. I recall a Cruise Director telling about a large inebriated man who undressed, put his clothing in his suitcase and his suitcase in the hall, then staggered to bed on the last night. In his strong Aussie accent, the Cruise Director described him as "four hundred pounds of lovin', he was." The guy had nothing but his whitey-tighties to wear off the ship the next morning! I've never personally seen a man disembark in his unmentionables, but on quite a few cruises, we've seen passengers wearing only a cruise line bathrobe and a sheepish expression making their way down the gangway. Oh, that bathrobe? Not complimentary, in either definition of the word.

More Luggage

You can **carry off your own bags on disembarkation day,** but it's a hassle. It's a chore to drag your overstuffed suitcases, shopping bags, piñatas, new hats, carry-on bags, and so on down the corridor, into the log jammed elevator, down the ramp, through the terminal, all the while dodging other people who had the same bright idea. Think about it...the root word of "luggage" is LUG. You paid for people to wrangle your Stuff—I say, let them!

A main reason people choose to haul their own bags is the fear of them getting lost and gone forever. This does happen, but very very rarely. Before reaching the ship, I **tape a luggage tag** flat against the side of my luggage, plus the one attached to the handle, as directed. I often add another on a second handle, just to be sure. Highly unlikely every one of them will be pulled off.

Worried about your luggage being overweight on the way home? That can happen, you know, if you did any shopping on your vacation! You can buy a small hand-held luggage scale, but you'll use it for only a few seconds. Better yet, ask your cabin steward for one. They often have a scale you can borrow. Extra airline fees are to be avoided whenever possible!

The More You Save, the More You Can Cruise

Compare costs accurately. A cruise looks pricey, until you think about what it includes. Transportation, a different place every day, lodging, a major show nightly, minor shows like comedians, professional dancers, and magicians, games, activities, live music, a dance floor, fancy and casual food 24 hours a day --and free room service (breakfast in bed is nice)--,scenery, quiet places, pools, hot tubs, things to do with other people, time to do nothing at all, on and on. It's nice not to think about where-are-we-staying-tonight, or we-spent-so-much-on-lunch; we'd-better-skip-dinner. Often, a per day cruise cost is less than a night at a Holiday Inn.

The Travel section of your Sunday newspaper often has colorful ads for the most exotic cruises ever, at unbelievable prices. Read the fine print...often, they are indeed not to be believed. Prices may be at odd times with heavy blackout dates, and may not even include the ports pictured. They're geared towards catching the eye of new cruisers. The ads often require you book expensive airfare through them, and they never mention fees such as taxes, fees, and port charges. Deals can be had this way, but you're often better on your own. Be careful to read the details before you book.

Remember that **cruise prices are per person, not per cabin.** Solo cruisers pay a surcharge, up to 200% of the fee. Much better to bring a friend! That way, it costs the same, but you only pay your part. It's also nice to be able to share experiences, and of course your stories are more believable if you have a witness.

Saving Money

Last Minute Cruises

The longest we've ever booked a cruise out was fourteen eternity-sized months, and the anticipation was miserable! I can pack in no time flat—you could time me—so 'let's book it and go' is my motto. I like **last minute cruises**.

The closest we've ever cut it was booking a cruise Tuesday evening, and it sailed that Saturday. We had a great time, and I reveled in knowing everyone else paid at least 80% more than we did. If you can be flexible, are not heartset on that one cabin and no other, and can handle the not-knowing, amazing deals can be had!

Actually, "last minute" in cruise line terms is **seventy-five to ninety days before sailing**, plenty of time for anticipating and planning a cruise. That's when final payment is due for passengers who booked on time, or very early, like some I could mention. The cabins not paid for in full at that date become available for resale. The cruise line's goal is to fill every ship, so these cabins often go for much less than their earlier price. The closer it gets to the sail date, the more anxious the cruise line is to fill the cabins, and the lower these cabins sell for. Of course, you'll not get the best selection of cabins, but **being flexible can save you hundreds of dollars.**

Upgrades

On a similar note, **ask about upgrades very close to your sailing.** If you can jump up a couple of categories for a few dollars, it's a great deal! You may not want to book an ocean view for $600 more per person at the time of booking, but if that cabin is still available nearer sailing, it could cost you $25 to upgrade. Take it! You can call the cruise line directly to inquire a few weeks before sailing date, or have your travel agent do it for you.

If you really are certain that only that specific cabin will do, **you might be better off booking far in advance.** Remember you can always change your mind and cancel if a better price comes along, up to the final payment date, seventy-five to ninety days before sailing. This gets you the best choice of cabins. You can change up to final payment date as many times as the price drops. It's like putting a bookmark in place; you're not obliged to finish the book.

Travel Agents

I recommend building a **relationship with a trusted Travel Agent,** preferably one with a brick–and –mortar office. Pick one who specializes in cruises; they often have sailed on the ships, and can speak from experience. They can do the legwork for you, as well as offer tips such as "you need a passport" and "it's mosquito season there; the next month is better."

If there is An Issue with the cruise line, a Travel Agent goes to bat for you. Ours also watches for price drops, and negotiates as needed. Husband (alias The Cruise Addict) happens to have our Travel Agent on speed dial. A good Travel Agent can make recommendations on ships and destinations, and suggest cruises that fit your personality and desires. Ours, for example, knows we are always on the lookout for a bargain on a great cruise. I am frugal, and Husband isn't called The Cruise Addict for nothing.

Shop around: we've heard of agents who charge for booking, or add fees for phone calls, and horror stories of agents who vanish after the initial booking abound. Ours is great, but I don't dare suggest him...he'd be too busy for us!

Discounts

Various discounts are available; see if you fit into the requirements when you book. **The cruise lines need to fill their ships to make money, and they reach out to different groups.** Discounts can include seniors (55 and older; sigh), union members, specific occupations such as teachers and police, AARP, past cruisers on that cruise line, <u>or</u> on a competitors' line, military members, stockholders in the cruise line, on and on. They even target residents of specific states. Nebraska has no seaport, thus Nebraskans less cruise than Floridians, who need no encouragement.

The discounts vary by time of year, itinerary, cruise line, ship, and the random whims of whoever decides these things. In any event, be sure to ask what discounts might apply when you book your cruise.

Is It about the Ship, or the Itinerary?

Are you more interested in the destination and ports, or the ship itself? Some people say "the ship IS the destination." I happen to disagree. I see a cruise ship as a delightful means to explore new places. If you're like me, take time to the various compare ships that have similar itineraries. It could make a big difference to you. For example, NCL is usually in Juneau only half a day, moving out so another NCL ship can berth there in the afternoon. Princess, on the other hand, is in Juneau for thirteen hours. NCL is currently the only line that has a cruise exclusively around Hawaii. In a seven day cruise, it has five ports, including two overnights. The other lines go out of southern California, with a very brief stop in Mexico. *Brief* I say; several stop in Ensenada for two hours! That's just long enough to meet the legal requirement for stopping in a foreign port, but not even long enough for passengers to get off the ship. They can have as many as nine sea days, with only three or four Hawaiian port days. Sea days can be pleasant, but is that really as much time as you want in the islands? On the other hand, back to back port days can be exhausting in places where ports are fairly close together. A couple of our cruises had ports so close, we could stand in one port, and see the next one. You don't want to feel like your trip is blurred together. Decide what is most important to you.

Extra Costs

And How To Save $$

Tips of 15%-20% are built into the spa services, as well as bar service. If you write in another tip on the line provided, it's double tipping. It's certainly fine if you want to do that, just be aware.

Understand how cruise lines make their money. They often LOSE money on the cabin booking alone. **Most of their revenue comes from sales of alcohol, shore excursions, casino and bingo**. You can certainly run up a huge onboard bill, but many passengers disembark with a zero balance, having had a fantastic vacation. We try to limit fancy drinks to one or two a day, but often, we find we ordered less than that! Seems we're always full from all the food...who feels like another froufrou drink?

Several cruise lines have gone to **mandatory Daily Service Charges**, or Prepaid Gratuities, which makes them not exactly tips anymore. Regardless of how they word it, be aware of this extra expense. Karma kicks in when you decide not to tip...regardless of your opinion of the tipping cultures, the crew members depend on tips as part to their income. You are blessed to be able to vacation. Don't quibble over a few dollars.

Unless you have a genuine problem--- in which case, reread the Complaining section.

Read even small things, like bar receipts. Of course, it's expected you'll tip someone who brings you a drink, but look closely. There's already a 15% tip added! By writing in a tip on the line provided, you're double tipping. Go ahead, if you want to, but it's certainly not expected.

Taxes and port charges are on top of the basic cruise fare, and never go on sale. Some ports are quite high, such as Brazil and Alaska, while others, like St Thomas, are much less. Compare, again; this could be a deal breaker for you.

Compare nearby airports, if you fly to a port. For example, Fort Lauderdale is often much less to fly into than Miami, and it's a short cab ride to the port. Flights out of Vancouver BC can be $400 more per person than out of Seattle. Taking a shuttle or Amtrak ($29 per person) to Seattle can be a huge savings. Los Angeles has five airports, and you can save considerable time money by choosing the ones closer to the ship's terminal. Not to mention the hassle of giant LAX!

Amtrak often offers discounts to port cities, if you travel within one day of a cruise. You'll need a cruise reservation number to request the discount, so book the ship first.

If you fly to a port, consider **a pre cruise hotel** near your home airport. Often, they offer stay-one-night-park-free-for-a-week deals, and that can save you a lot over parking at the airport. Often hotels have a free shuttle to the airport, too.

Parking at the terminal is very expensive. Look into options for **off-site parking** if you drive to the port. Again, call a nearby hotel to see if they offer cheaper long-term parking.

 Be open to alternative transportation. In Los Angeles, saw a sign on concierge's desk at the hotel: "Shuttle to Pier $10." Wow—a taxi would have cost triple that! We booked it, showed up at the requested time, and were surprised to see the "shuttle" was actually a stretch limousine! Very nice way to start our cruise.

We lucked out like that another time, too; Husband (alias The Cruise Addict) found a limo company that would give the six of us a four- hour tour before taking us to   the airport for *$165 less* than a shuttle bus from cruise terminal to airport directly. I appreciated the savings, but the real fun was seeing our granddaughter's face light up when she realized the shiny stretch limo pulling up, was for us!

Should You Bundle?

Cruise lines sell packages with flights and cruise combined into one price. **This is very rarely a good idea.** Yes, it's a little bit easier; they wrangle your luggage, a bus meets you at the airport and takes you directly to the ship, and you don't have to hassle with booking your own flights. However, the tradeoff is that you go when the cruise line says you go, often on less than ideal flights, with multiple layovers or at odd times, and you have no control over when you arrive in the port. Usually the combination will cost significantly more than booking it yourself.

A random thought...I'm not big on standing in lines. If you arrive at the port the same time as everyone else who did the same thing as you, you've brought your own line of people to wait in!

Personally, I've heard nothing but complaints from people who have taken these deals. I think it's much better to book your own vacation, to shop for the best price at a time that suits you, and of course, arriving a day or so early allows more play time in the departure city. We book our own flights to and from the pier. We have more control over times, flights, airlines, and seats, plus it costs a whole lot less than paying the cruise line put you on any old flight. And we can board the ship when we get there, not dependent on a bus schedule.

Repositioning Cruises

Repositioning cruises can be a bargain! Ships are always in the best places in the best weather, so they move ships around as seasons change. For example, ships are in the Mediterranean, Caribbean, Mexico and Hawaii in the winter, then those same ships move to Alaska, northern Europe, and Scandinavia in the summer months. As the ship moves to the new place, the routes are only one way, ending in a different port. Ships might go from California to Vancouver, to start the Alaska season, or from New England to the Bahamas. We've enjoyed exploring new ships as we've taken one- and three-day Northwest cruises on the "shoulder" season trips.

Obviously, these routes are only once a year, then back again when the season turns. **You can get very good prices on repositioning cruises!** Be sure to factor in one way airfare home... we keep drooling over astonishingly low cruise fares from New York to Europe, until we figured that airfare back home would cost more than the fifteen -day cruise. Someday...

Loyalty Pays Off

Every cruise line has a **loyalty program** of some sort. Join them! The programs are free, and can net you some bonuses down the road. Perks include notification of special sales, newsletters/magazines, cabin upgrades, treats in your cabin, invitation to members-only parties, priority boarding, ship tours, onboard credit, bottles of wine, free dinners in specialty restaurants on board, small discounts on photos and gift shop purchases, all for free. Some cruise lines require you to sign up, while others are automatic on your first cruise.

Every cruise line has a mailing list, and they are happy to send you colorful brochures with maps and sailing itineraries. These are a fine way to look at what they offer, but ignore the prices. It's like buying a new car; only a dunderhead pays list prices. Get on the mailing lists of cruise lines you might be interested in eventually.

Be brand-loyal. Stick to one cruise line, because perks add up fast for frequent cruisers. Free drinks, free laundry , free internet , specialty restaurant dinners, free spa treatments, free wine and snacks in your cabin, and advance notification of sales, are all possibilities and can rack up considerable savings.

Don't be brand-loyal. Open mindedness on cruise lines can often net better deals, and often diverse itineraries, plus a new and different experience. Compare before you book---there are a lot of choices. Wouldn't you feel bad if there is another cruise line out there that's even better, goes awesome places with great itineraries, and costs the same or less than the one you love? We met some cruisers who were so brand loyal, they would not consider another cruise line! They didn't even know what other ships had to offer. Options are good!

One of the great things about a cruise vacation that it's different and exciting every time. That's harder if you go to the same places on the same ship over and over. You will very likely enjoy cruising, and if you do, spread your wings a little. We know people who even book the *same cabin* every time!

HAPPY CRUISING!!

Useful Websites:

Cruisebuzz.com

CruiseCritic.com

CruiseMates.com

Cruise.com

CruiseDeals.com

BudgetTravel.com

RoyalCaribbean.com

CelebrityCruises.com

NCL.com

Carnival.com

Disneycruise.disney.go.com/

Princess.com

HollandAmerica.com

BONUS SECTION:

Advice Directly from The Cruise Addict Himself :

There are several ways to snag a good deal on a cruise. The websites that advertise Amazing last minute deals usually are not one of them. Most of the cruise lines, a couple of years back, started making the sites like Travelocity, Orbitz and Expedia use the same price that the cruise lines' own sites gave. That stopped the travel sites from discounting cruises and undercutting the cruise lines. So when you look up the price on one site it is the same price on all of the others. They can still give out perks like free wine, dinners, and onboard credit.

Some local travel agents will buy a block of rooms and be able to discount the price that way. When they buy eight rooms they get one room free. The travel agents will send out an email with a unadvertised specials. They will not post these deals on their webpage so the cruise line will not get upset.

Also some of the cruise lines send out specials to those customers that are in their loyalty program. These deals never make it to the internet and are only for those customers that have sailed on that cruise line before. These programs are free to join.

With every rule there are some exceptions. Sometimes a cruise line will let one of the major sites discount a particular cruise and nobody else gets the deal. This is very rare, but worth checking.

Cruises are less expensive if you travel in the early spring or late autumn. Anytime you have children in school, the lines do not charge as much, because most families travel in the summer and school holidays like Christmas and Spring Break. An early February cruise could be as little as half the price as a summer one. When dealing with places like Alaska, May and September will be the least expensive months.

When you book your cruise, your work is not done. Keep watching the price the cruise line is selling similar cabins for now. Sometimes the price of the room goes down. If it is before final payment then you can cancel and rebook the new cabin and get the discount or negotiate the discount and stay in your current room. They can also give you an onboard credit in place of a discount. I like working with a travel agent for this part. They will do the negotiating for you.

If it is after final payment, it is harder to squeeze a discount out of a line but sometimes they will upgrade you if you ask. On our last cruise we able to upgrade from an inside to an ocean view and the cruise line gave us $250.00 back. The price had gone down that much.

So my tips are:

#1 Get on as many cruise line mailing lists as possible. You will get a lot of email, and pretty brochures in your mailbox, but you will always be in the know about upcoming deals. If it bothers you, make a new email address, just for cruise email.

#2 Always register for a cruise line's loyalty program as soon as you take the first cruise on that line.

#3 Once you have decided on a cruise, check other web sites for a better price. Comparing can save you a bundle.

#4 Travel in the Early Spring or late Fall when the kids are in school for the best prices.

#5 Keep checking prices after you book.

#6 Find a trusted travel agent, and build a relationship with them.

When we got an email from our travel agent with a cruise deal that was half the normal price, we jumped. He had a special rate he had gotten through the cruise line and was passing along the savings. We booked a balcony cabin for $649. The current prices for the same balcony are $1149 so we are saving $500 a person. That is a total savings of $1000!

When we booked our Hawaii cruise we got a $799 special because we were part of the cruise line's loyalty program. Normally that cruise would have been $1149 for an inside cabin. Then we got a call and the cruise line offered us a balcony cabin for $100 extra. So we got a balcony for $700 less than an inside and $1950 less than what we should have paid for a balcony cabin. It's enough to get a person addicted to cruising.

Happy Cruising!

A Shameless Plea:

Thanks for taking time to read my book---you'll be a much smarter cruiser because of it! By following my tips, you can easily save hundreds of dollars, plus you'll be one of the most-informed people on any cruise ship.

I hope you'll pay me back. I would very, very, very much appreciate a 5-star review on the review page! I read every single review, and the 5 star ones absolutely make my day. Week! Five star reviews are a really big deal, like leaving a $100 tip for your cabin steward. It will take you under three minutes to write a one-line 5 star review, and you can do it anonymously if you wish. It means a lot to me. Tell your friends! Thanks so much!!

thecruiseaddictswife@ yahoo.com

Think about taking

disposable underwater camera

snorkeling mask

waterproof container for valuables swimming

cheap thin rain ponchos

Think about getting ready

cruise critic online forum for this cruise

prepare envelopes for each stop (port)